JOURNAL FOR THE STUDY OF THE OLD TESTAMENT
SUPPLEMENT SERIES

95

Editors
David J A Clines
Philip R Davies

JSOT Press
Sheffield

GOD SAVES

Lessons from the
Elisha Stories

Rick Dale Moore

Journal for the Study of the Old Testament
Supplement Series 95

Copyright © 1990 Sheffield Academic Press

Published by JSOT Press
JSOT Press is an imprint of
Sheffield Academic Press Ltd
The University of Sheffield
343 Fulwood Road
Sheffield S10 3BP
England

Printed on acid free-paper in Great Britain
by Billing & Sons Ltd
Worcester

British Library Cataloguing in Publication Data

Moore, Rick Dale
 God saves: lessons from the Elisha stories.
 1. Bible. O.T. Kings - Critical studies
 I. Title II. Series
 222.506

ISSN 0309-0787
ISBN 1-85075-259-1

CONTENTS

Preface 7
Abbreviations 9

Chapter 1
CLASSIFYING THE ELISHA STORIES 11
   Introduction 11
   Hermann Gunkel's Foundational Work 12
   The Extension of Gunkel's Approach 20
   Departures from Gunkel's Approach 34
   Summary 63

Chapter 2
THE THREE ELISHA STORIES IN
LITERARY-AESTHETIC PERSPECTIVE 69
   Introduction 69
   2 Kings 5.1-27 71
   2 Kings 6.8-23 84
   2 Kings 6.24–7.20 95

Chapter 3
THE THREE ELISHA STORIES IN
CONTEXTUAL PERSPECTIVE 105
   Introduction 105
   Prophetic Veneration 106
   Prophetic Conflict 111
   Conflict with Baalism 117
   Class Conflict 121
   Theological Struggle with Aramean Domination 128

Chapter 4
CONCLUSION 149

Bibliography 153
Index of Biblical References 163
Index of Authors 167

PREFACE

Many valued teachers, colleagues, friends, and family members have contributed vitally to the completion of this project. Several of them deserve special mention.

First, to my teachers at Vanderbilt University I wish to express my sincere appreciation. I am especially indebted to Professors Crenshaw, Harrelson, and Knight for their expert guidance and kind encouragement along the way. I also owe special thanks to Dorothy Parks, Director of the Divinity Library, whose help and friendship thoughout my program will not be forgotten.

Second, I wish to thank my friends and colleagues of Cleveland, Tennessee, with whom I work and worship. Their prayers and support have been invaluable. I especially thank Peter Thomas and Michael DeLong for helping me through some difficult German, and also Chuck Sherrill and Jewel Frazier for their technical help on the first two chapters.

Third, to my family members, who have deeply and freely shared in this burden, I wish to return my deepest gratitude and blessing. I extend heart-felt thanks to my wife's parents, Jim and Margaret Hamilton, who have been a tremendous source of financial and moral support to me and my family. I owe inexpressible thanks to my parents, Buel and Doris Moore, whose early guidance in the Word of God has been an enduring inspiration and anchor, and to my wife Jean and our two daughters, Emily and Hannah, whose companionship has been the daily strength and joy, without which this work never could have been done.

Finally, I should like to express my thanks to Professor David Clines for his acceptance of my work into the JSOT Supplement Series, and for his detailed editing and proofreading of the final manuscript.

Spanning across and beyond all of this valued help I must

finally thank my Lord, whose salvation, about which I have here written, has marvelously appeared to me.

ABBREVIATIONS

AfO	*Archiv für Orientforschung*
ATANT	Abhandlungen zur Theologie des Alten und Neuen Testaments
ATD	Das Alte Testament Deutsch
AV	Authorized Version
BA	*The Biblical Archaeologist*
BASOR	*Bulletin of the American Schools of Oriental Research*
BHS	Biblia Hebraica Stuttgartensia
BR	*Biblical Research*
BWANT	Beiträge zur Wissenschaft vom Alten und Neuen Testament
BZAW	Beihefte zur Zeitschrift für die alttestamentliche Wissenschaft
CBQ	*Catholic Biblical Quarterly*
DLZ	*Deutsche Literaturzeitung*
EvT	*Evangelische Theologie*
ExpTim	*Expository Times*
FRLANT	Forschungen zur Religion und Literatur des Alten und Neuen Testaments
HKAT	Handkommentar zum Alten Testament
HSM	Harvard Semitic Monographs
HTR	*Harvard Theological Review*
IDB	*Interpreter's Dictionary of the Bible*
IDBSup	*Supplementary Volume to IDB*
Int	*Interpretation*
JNES	*Journal of Near Eastern Studies*
JSOT	*Journal for the Study of the Old Testament*
JSOTS	Journal for the Study of the Old Testament Supplement Series
JTC	*Journal for Theology and the Church*
JTS	*Journal of Theological Studies*

KdG	Kultur der Gegenwart
MT	Masoretic Text
NASB	New American Standard Bible
NEB	New English Bible
NedTTS	*Nederlands theologische tijdschrift*
NIV	New International Version
OTS	*Oudtestamentische Studiën*
RevScRel	*Revue des sciences religieuses*
RGG	*Die Religion in Geschichte und Gegenwart*
RSR	*Recherches de science religieuse*
RSV	Revised Standard Version
SANT	Studien zum Alten und Neuen Testament
SAT	Die Schriften des Alten Testaments
SBLDS	Society of Biblical Literature Dissertation Series
SBLMS	Society of Biblical Literature Monograph Series
SBT	Studies in Biblical Theology
SR	Studies in Religion/Sciences Religieuses
TB	Theologische Bücherei
TLZ	*Theologische Literaturzeitung*
VT	*Vetus Testamentum*
VTS	Vetus Testamentum Supplements
WMANT	Wissenschaftliche Monographien zum Alten und Neuen Testament
ZAW	Zeitschrift für die alttestamentliche Wissenschaft
ZTK	Zeitschrift für Theologie und Kirche

Chapter 1

CLASSIFYING THE ELISHA STORIES

Introduction

This book grows out of a conviction that the three Elisha stories found in 2 Kings 5, 6.8-23, and 6.24–7.20 have not been adequately understood. The present chapter, which establishes the background for my own fresh examination, reviews the studies which have played a key role in shaping the scholarly understanding of these three narratives. The particular line of research which I will review here concerns the way the given stories have been categorized and classified. The classification of these stories has been the controlling issue in their interpretation since the time of Hermann Gunkel. But the chief problem with this effort has been the tendency to reach conclusions about the generic function of these stories before sufficient attention has been paid to their specific features and dynamics.

As we shall see, the very general classifications of Gunkel, which have dominated for most of this century, were the product much more of his broad presuppositions concerning the development of Hebrew literature than of any detailed analysis of the biblical narratives themselves. Several scholars who have judged Gunkel's classifications inadequate in representing the specifics of the biblical narratives have initiated new approaches which see these specifics as the necessary starting point for determining generic function. As the following review will show, the efforts in this vein, in relation to these particular Elisha stories, have been flawed by the tendency to stress certain aspects of the biblical text to the neglect of others. In the following chapters I hope to show that a new understanding of the meaning and function of the narratives is possible when a full range of internal features and external factors is brought into focus.

It should be noted that, both in the present review of research and in the analysis which follows, I am concerned with these stories in their independent integrity rather than with their current disposition within the so-called Deuteronomistic History. This focus upon the predeuteronomistic level of composition involves a confidence that, despite the fact that these stories have passed through editorial hands, the prior form of the respective stories has not been obfuscated. While the collection of prophetical stories may have been editorially interrupted, the earlier form of the individual stories has not been disrupted. This confidence is supported by the leading scholarly treatments of the compositional history of the deuteronomistic complex.[1]

The classification of particular Elisha narratives has not taken place apart from the classification of prophetical narratives generally. Thus, the path we trace here will not only give us a key vantage on the entire body of research on our narratives, but it will also bring this wider circle of biblical study within our field of vision, allowing us to see how classification of these stories might have implications for a wider range of narratives.

Hermann Gunkel's Foundational Work

The work of Hermann Gunkel is the right place to begin a survey of the effort to classify the three main Elisha stories found in 2 Kings 5–7. As the leading pioneer of biblical form criticism, Gunkel established the basic categories by which not only these three stories but all biblical literature came to be

---

1 See Martin Noth, *The Deuteronomistic History* (trans. J. Doull *et al.*; JSOTS, 15; Sheffield: JSOT, 1981), pp. 71-72 (originally published in German in 1943); Rudolf Smend, 'Das Gesetz und die Völker: Ein Beitrag zur deuteronomistischen Redaktionsgeschichte', *Probleme Biblischer Theologie: Gerhard von Rad zum 70. Geburtstag* (ed. H.W. Wolff; Munich: Chr. Kaiser, 1971), pp. 500-509; Walter Dietrich, *Prophetie und Geschichte: Eine redaktionsgeschichtliche Untersuchung zum deuteronomistischen Geschichtswerk* (FRLANT, 108; Göttingen: Vandenhoeck & Ruprecht, 1972), p. 46; Richard D. Nelson, *The Double Redaction of the Deuteronomistic History* (JSOTS, 18; Sheffield: JSOT, 1981), pp. 110-12.

1. Classifying the Elisha Stories   13

viewed. Gunkel's ground-breaking work on biblical narrative came in his commentary on Genesis published in 1901.[1] Working from the specific pericopes of Genesis, Gunkel outlined a typology which became the base point for classifying all biblical narratives, prophetical stories included. While not exhaustive in itself, this typology provided an authoritative foundation from which there could be extended application, amplification and emendation by others as well as by Gunkel himself.

It was not Gunkel's direct comment on these Elisha narratives which accounts for his dominating influence on their subsequent classification. Gunkel published a monograph on the Elisha narratives some years after his commentary on Genesis,[2] but he expressed himself no more specifically on the matter of the literary form of these narratives than to call them sagas.[3] As indicated in his introduction, Gunkel's main aim here was rather to highlight the beauty and originality of their narrative artistry.[4] Gunkel's lasting impact on the classification of these narratives came more indirectly by way of the subsequent appropriation and extension of his system of narrative categories.

As I have mentioned, Gunkel's identification of the Elisha stories as sagas did not represent any very specific typological designation. However, it is needful to begin our look at Gunkel's typology with saga precisely because it stands at the

---

1 *Genesis* (HKAT, I/1; Göttingen: Vandenhoeck & Ruprecht, 1901).
2 *Geschichten von Elisa* (Meisterwerke hebräischer Erzählungskunst, 1; Berlin: Karl Curtius [1925]).
3 I use 'saga' to translate the German term *Sage*, as has become the most common practice in translations and in works written in English. This leaves the word 'legend' to translate the German term *Legende*, avoiding the unfortunate confusion seen in the English translation of Gunkel's study of the *Sagen* of Genesis: *The Legends of Genesis* (trans. W.H. Carruth; Chicago: Open Court, 1901). I am aware of the recent scholarly objections to the common usage and application of these German and English terms (e.g. John J. Scullion, '*Märchen, Sage, Legende*: Towards a Clarification of Some Literary Terms Used by Old Testament Scholars', *VT* 34 [1984], pp. 321-60); however, my purpose at this point is to represent the general scholarly discussion and not any of my own proposals for form-critical precision.
4 *Elisa*, pp. 1-2.

head of his analysis of biblical narrative categories. Saga was the inclusive category used by Gunkel to distinguish the kind of writings found in the book of Genesis from history writing. In his introduction to *Genesis*, the distinction between saga and history writing was set forth in a series of contrasts: (1) oral vs written transmission, (2) private vs public subject matter, (3) basis in tradition and imagination vs witnesses and records, (4) inclusion of the miraculous and improbable vs restriction to the credible and probable, and (5) poetical and inspirational intent vs prosaic and informational aim.[1]

After marking off the broad category of saga, Gunkel acknowledged that the stories of Genesis suggested some subdivisions. Gunkel first made a division in terms of the specific biblical material itself, distinguishing the primeval narratives (Gen. 1–11) from the patriarchal narratives (Gen. 12–50). From this point, however, Gunkel shifted to a more formal and generic identification of these and further subdivisions, using abstract taxonomy and terms. Gunkel identified the narratives of the first part of Genesis as mythical sagas, pointing up their similarities to Near Eastern myth, while acknowledging their monotheistic distinctiveness.[2] In his work on the patriarchal sagas, Gunkel marked out lines of classification which were relevant to the remaining narratives of Genesis but which also opened up toward the wider corpus of Old Testament narratives. The three saga-types given prominence in this part of Gunkel's discussion were (1) historical sagas, defined in terms of their dependence upon some historical occurrence, (2) ethnographic sagas, characterized by their depiction of relations between tribes and peoples, and (3) etiological sagas, identified by their aim to explain something, usually in terms of its origin.[3] The ethnographic and etiological sagas understandably had primary significance for Genesis. However, the historical saga, the type least represented in Genesis, was to have the greatest amount of impact in classifying biblical narratives beyond the book of

---

1 Gunkel, *The Legends of Genesis* (trans. W.H. Carruth, reissued with an introduction by William F. Albright; New York: Schocken Books, 1964), pp. 3-12.
2 *Legends*, pp. 15-18.
3 *Op. cit.*, pp. 24-25.

1. Classifying the Elisha Stories

Genesis. The expanding relevance of historical saga to Old Testament narratives beyond Genesis is reflected in the fact that, when Gunkel moved beyond his initial focus on Genesis, he elevated historical saga to a major category alongside patriarchal saga, rather than continuing to treat it as a sub-type of the latter.[1]

Interestingly, Gunkel began to refer to historical sagas alternatively, as *Volkshelden* sagas, sagas of folk heroes.[2] Without setting aside the earlier term (*historische Sagen*) or its description, he began to characterize the central focus in this narrative type in terms of historical personages significant to the community. This emphasis followed naturally, it seems, from Gunkel's way of seeing patriarchal sagas as the developmental antecedent of historical sagas, with a focus on archetypal ancestors in the former being seen to give way to a focus on historical figures in the latter.[3] In discussions which did not move beyond broad strokes, Gunkel ranged Elisha among the primary folk heroes whom he associated with the category of historical saga.[4]

It is significant that whereas saga as a general category had earlier been defined largely by distinction from history, historical saga was identified precisely by its link to history. This created an ambiguous relationship between the historical saga and historical writing. Yet the ambiguity is explained, once again, by the developmental relationship which Gunkel perceived between the two narrative categories. Gunkel saw the historical saga as the direct literary antecedent of historical writing,[5] so that one would expect some such pivotal connection between them. However, this continuity at the boundary understandably led Gunkel to devote much of his discussion to

---

1 *Die israelitische Literatur* (Darmstadt: Wissenschaftliche Buchgesellschaft, 1963), pp. 19-21. This work first appeared as an article in *Die orientalischen Literaturen* (ed. P. Hinneberg; KdG, 1/7; Leipzig: B.G. Teubner, 1906), pp. 53-112.
2 *Ibid.*
3 'Sagen und Legenden: II. In Israel', *RGG* (2nd edn, 1931), V, col. 53.
4 *Op. cit.*, col. 54.
5 *Op. cit.*, col. 53. See also *Die israelitische Literatur*, p. 23.

pressing the distinction between historical saga and historical writing. Here he emphasized how the historical saga freely augments historical memories with imaginary embellishments.[1] Gunkel saw in this what one might describe as Israel's impulse to recall its heroes with both more immanence and more transcendence than the historical record itself would have provided. That is, on the one hand, Israel's public heroes are brought near through imaginative representation of their private lives, while on the other hand, these characters are constantly being drawn larger than life with the use of numerous miraculous elements.

The miraculous elements of historical saga point ahead to one other category of Gunkel's typology which, after Gunkel, came to be important for classifying prophetical stories—the legend (*Legende*). Gunkel perceived the legend as a late offshoot from historical saga.[2] Legend was like saga in highlighting a heroic figure, but Gunkel felt that the legend pursued spiritual lessons and miraculous themes to the point of showing less interest in real personalities and events. This definition pointed to no clear-cut elements or features in the legend which marked it off decisively from the saga, since saga too was largely defined by its standing apart from history with spiritual and supernatural dimensions. Still Gunkel ascribed to legend a changed 'tone' and a 'peculiarly spiritual' quality.[3] He described this along the lines of a narrow religious focus which tended to lack the earlier aesthetic sense and its delight in the past for its own sake. Yet even here no discrete and decisive literary indicators are offered. We are left with less of a boundary here than was the case between historical saga and historical writing. However, Gunkel probably gave some substance to the identity of legend by placing it as a post-exilic development.[4] Whereas saga was, in a literal sense, a prehistorical development, legend came only later, emerging over against a developed historical consciousness. Thus, while it remained difficult to see any clear difference between legend

---

1 'Sagen und Legenden', col. 54.
2 *Op. cit.*, col. 58.
3 *Ibid.*
4 *Ibid.* See also *Die israelitische Literatur*, pp. 46-47.

1. Classifying the Elisha Stories 17

and historical saga, developmentally these narrative types could be understood as moving in opposite directions in relation to historicity, with the historical saga being seen as moving toward it and the legend as moving away from it. Here again, the developmental relationship between categories which are defined largely by their relation to historicity seems to have played a decisive role in Gunkel's own discrimination.

It hardly appears that Gunkel's perception of the developmental relationship between categories existed merely to serve his typology. In fact, if anything Gunkel's attempt to reconstruct a history of Israelite literature (*Literaturgeschichte*)[1] tended in his work on narrative to take precedence over his delineation of literary forms (*Gattungsforschung*). Thus, while it is true that Gunkel's developmental approach served to enhance the otherwise scant identity of his narrative types, we should also recognize that the scant definitions of Gunkel's narrative types served his desire to see them in terms of a developmental scheme. Simple, one-dimensional definitions went hand-in-hand with the attempt to plot a linear progression between categories. In this last point we encounter the evolutionary thinking which runs so deeply in Gunkel's work and that of his generation.[2] The decades of scholarship since Gunkel have made his developmentalism appear rather simplistic and naive, whether we are speaking about his approach in general[3] or his specific way of schematizing narratives on the basis of their relation to historicity. The criterion of historicity now appears much more like the preoccupation of the modern interpreter than the governing criterion of the ancient writer.[4] At any rate, it is important to

---

1 Gunkel's first programmatic statement of this attempt was given in *Die israelitische Literatur*. See also his 'Fundamental Problems of Hebrew Literary History', in *What Remains of the Old Testament? And Other Essays* (trans. A.K. Dallas; New York: Macmillan, 1928), pp. 57-68.
2 On this, see the helpful survey of Herbert F. Hahn, *The Old Testament in Modern Research* (Philadelphia: Fortress, 1966), pp. 8-10, 46.
3 See, e.g. J.W. Rogerson, *Anthropology and the Old Testament* (Atlanta: John Knox, 1978), pp. 43-44.
4 So Otto Kaiser, *Introduction to the Old Testament* (trans. John Sturdy; Minneapolis: Augsburg, 1977), p. 51.

recognize the interdependence of Gunkel's developmentalism and his classification of narratives.

It might be helpful at this point to summarize Gunkel's work as it relates to classifying stories from the Elisha cycle. While Gunkel, in the monograph he devoted to the Elisha stories, classified them only as sagas, it is clear from his more general discussions that he saw the subdivision of historical saga or hero saga as applying to them.[1] The fact that Gunkel does not make use of this more specific classification in his concentrated study of the Elisha stories is curious. Yet it may help to point up the fact that this subdivision remained so general as to be of limited relevance to a more detailed scrutiny of these stories.

The need for more specific narrative classifications seemed not to be felt by Gunkel. He made an apparent gesture in this direction in his treatment of patriarchal sagas in his original work on Genesis, but what at first looks like a suggestion for more specific saga types finally shows itself to be no more than a reference to various saga motifs.[2] Indeed, identifying various saga motifs emerged as one of the two tacks by which Gunkel addressed sagas in terms of greater specificity; the other was recognizing what he referred to as different 'styles'.[3] Thus, in his famous article in *RGG*, Gunkel included after his presentation of the three main saga types a discussion of saga motifs and styles.[4] The intent of Gunkel's discussion here appears to have been illustrative rather than comprehensive. On the subject of motifs, he mentioned only etiological motifs, within which category he differentiated etymological, ethnographic and ceremonial motifs, offering a smattering of examples for each. On the subject of styles, his analysis was even more cursory. He contrasted a simple, unadorned saga style, which he associated with sagas in their primitive, oracular cast, with whatever degree of literary elaboration beyond the saga's bare elements.

What Gunkel viewed as style actually incorporated what he

1 See the comments above on p.15.
2 *Legends*, pp. 34-35. This point is acknowledged by Kaiser, *Introduction*, pp. 48-49.
3 'Sagen und Legenden', cols. 55-56.
4 *Ibid.*

1. Classifying the Elisha Stories

discussed under motifs. Both in the *RGG* article[1] and in his *Die israelitische Literatur*[2] it seems that Gunkel saw style as a matter of the extent to which a simple saga had been augmented by saga motifs or even other sagas. Style, then, seemed to have less to do with outright literary creation than with the process of compiling or combining pre-existent saga traditions and motifs. Style developed, Gunkel surmised, as storytellers freely fashioned increasingly elaborate composites from the stock of materials deriving from the common lore.

Here again we see the developmental dimension of Gunkel's thought. Just as saga types were related in a developmental progression, saga style was seen in terms of a line of development from simple to complex. We saw that the developmental relation between types influenced the tendency to define the types in simple, general terms. This tendency was reinforced by Gunkel's developmental view of saga style. By seeing a correlation between simplicity of style and purity of saga type, Gunkel could explain any literary complexity as a matter of style without considering the possibility of more specialized saga types. Types, seen as the products of primitive folk conventions, could be defined by their general subject matter while the more specific content could be discussed in terms of the subsequent style of individual artistry which gave narrative types their dress without fundamentally affecting or informing their constitutive patterns.[3]

The specific traditions and motifs constituting style, then, were seen to cut across the main saga types, manifesting themselves and combining with one another in amorphous ways which yielded no further specification of classes. Gunkel showed no inclination to seek further typicality here, for he saw such fluidity as a vital aspect of the artistic freedom of the individual poetic personalities which he credited with this aspect of the sagas. A clear current of romanticism shows itself at this point.

It follows from what has just been said that leaving his saga

---

1 *Op. cit.*, col. 56.
2 Pp. 18-19.
3 Coming close to this observation is Martin J. Buss, 'The Study of Forms', ch. 1 in *Old Testament Form Criticism* (ed. John H. Hayes; San Antonio: Trinity University Press, 1977), p. 54.

classifications extremely general actually served and was served by Gunkel's romantic interpretation of the literary specifics of sagas. This helps to explain the approach Gunkel took in his detailed treatment of the Elisha stories, where he set for himself the task of exploring 'the originality and the special beauty' of these stories without identifying them more specifically than as sagas. It also helps to explain why his treatment of the specific literary content of these sagas led to no further detection or refinement of literary types but instead tended to be rather fragmented and fragmenting; for in exploring literary artistry, Gunkel was not really looking for more than a conglomeration of motifs and traditions, and this is precisely what he found.

It becomes easier to see why the further designation of the Elisha stories as *historical* sagas, which Gunkel indicated elsewhere, was ignored in his detailed treatment of these stories. Further typological specification was not wanted or needed to open up the detailed workings of specific narratives. For this, Gunkel looked to a romantic view of artistic spontaneity which further classification, if pursued, could only infringe upon.

The Extension of Gunkel's Approach

A key person in the extension of Gunkel's form-critical work on Old Testament narrative was Hugo Gressmann. Some have viewed Gressmann's role as that more of a co-founder than of a follower.[1] Certainly Gressmann and Gunkel worked closely together and represented the same basic narrative typology and approach. Yet while Gressmann seems to have influenced the formative process at some points, particularly with respect to the earlier narratives of the Old Testament, upon which he focused his early work,[2] Gressmann's work clearly followed Gunkel's lead overall and especially with

---

1 See Jay A. Wilcoxen, 'Narrative', ch. 2 in *Old Testament Form Criticism*, p. 58.
2 H. Gressmann, 'Sage und Geschichte in den Patriarchenerzählungen', ZAW 30 (1910), pp. 1-34; *Mose und seine Zeit: Ein Kommentar zu den Mose-Sagen* (FRLANT, 18; Göttingen: Vandenhoeck & Ruprecht, 1913).

1. Classifying the Elisha Stories

respect to the later literature, about which we are concerned. That part of Gressmann's work which related to classification of the Elisha stories appeared in a commentary in *Die Schriften des Alten Testaments*, covering material from Samuel to Amos.[1] In an introduction which treated the emergence of history-writing in Israel, Gressmann discussed saga, historical narrative, and legend along the lines laid out by Gunkel. Gressmann observed the same developmental progression from saga to history-writing and likewise saw legend as an offshoot of saga.[2] The distinctions drawn between these categories paralleled Gunkel's but included a few of Gressmann's own clarifying touches. For instance, Gressmann drew out history-writing's focus upon the present or near past as opposed to the saga's focus upon the distant past.[3] Despite such clarifications, Gressmann registered a significant admission—that the boundaries of saga and history-writing are fluid and that these classifications cannot always be applied with exactitude.[4] Perhaps the context of Gressmann's discussion—a commentary on the biblical text rather than an exposition of the typology—made Gressmann more sensitive to this fact.

The most significant difference in Gressmann's approach involved his view that the development from saga to history-writing could, and at times did, go the other way. He explained that a transition from history-writing to saga happened quite naturally out of the impulse to enhance actual happenings with the passing of time.[5] Gunkel was certainly keen on this impulse, but he connected it strictly with the legend, and one suspects that his evolutionary tendencies would have resisted any such direct reversal in his developmental scheme. Gressmann, however, seems to have held a much less schematic view of literary development. Rather than seeing the changes in Israel's literary history so much in terms of some inevitable cultural progression, Gressmann connected these changes

1 *Die älteste Geschichtsschreibung und Prophetie Israels* (SAT, 2/1; 2nd edn; Göttingen: Vandenhoeck & Ruprecht, 1921).
2 *Op. cit.*, pp. xiii-xv.
3 *Op. cit.*, pp. xiii-xiv.
4 *Op. cit.*, p. xiv.
5 *Ibid.*

much more closely to the vicissitudes of Israel's history. Thus, history-writing was seen to have been natural during the emergence of the monarchy, since the political events evoked a consciousness of things present, whereas the stable time of Solomon was seen to have facilitated the far-past orientation of saga.[1] The net effect of such thinking was to loosen the temporal distinctions Gunkel had used in differentiating his types, thereby permitting greater temporal flexibility in their application.

The foregoing helps explain Gressmann's specific classifications of the Elisha stories covered in his commentary in 2 Kings 5–7. While ch. 5 and 6.24–7.20 were designated as sagas, in agreement with Gunkel's classification, 6.8-23 was designated as a legend.[2] This classification seemed tied in no way to the story's having a post-exilic setting, as Gunkel would have insisted, but rather just to the story's sharpened edificatory thrust and increased separation from historical reality.[3]

Gressmann extended Gunkel's work in narrative classification by adopting Gunkel's typology and at points even tightening his definitions. Significantly, however, Gressmann loosened the developmental scheme put forward by Gunkel. He appreciated a historical variability in Israel's literary developments which allowed him a bit more flexibility in classification.

One way to trace the continuing sway of Gunkel's approach in the classification of the Old Testament prophetical stories in general and the Elisha stories in particular is to look at the most influential Old Testament introductions published after Gunkel. Most prominent among these was that of Otto Eissfeldt.[4]

Eissfeldt laid out a systematic presentation of Old Testament literary types following Gunkel's categories and nomenclature quite closely. Unlike Gunkel, however, Eissfeldt

---

1 *Ibid.*
2 *Op. cit.*, pp. 295-304.
3 *Op. cit.*, p. 300.
4 *The Old Testament: An Introduction* (trans. Peter R. Ackroyd; New York: Harper & Row, 1965). The original German edition first appeared in 1934.

1. Classifying the Elisha Stories 23

lacked the concern to trace the historical development of the literary types and their developmental relation to one another. Stressing the persistence of types through time, Eissfeldt's recognition of the historical perspective was minimal.[1] Thus his typology followed a topical rather than a chronological order.

One does not sense in Eissfeldt's presentation the stress on distinguishing and demarcating categories which was evident in Gunkel's work. The emphasis of Eissfeldt seems to have been upon application and illustration rather than qualification of categories. One meets the spirit of a guide who confidently surveys things taken to be well established. When one comes specifically to Eissfeldt's discussion and application of the narrative categories with which we have been concerned, it is clear that Eissfeldt showed a readiness to exploit rather than an impulse to redress the loose passage between these categories.

Eissfeldt found the categories of saga, legend and historical narrative *all* relevant to the classification of the Elisha stories.[2] This did not follow from any change which Eissfeldt was observing in the basic constitution of these types, for Eissfeldt showed no disagreement with Gunkel on this score.[3] On the other hand, Eissfeldt's ignoring the chronological and developmental distinctions which Gunkel had stressed gave him more freedom to apply these types in a fluid way and to appreciate the fluidity between them. The most significant result of this was Eissfeldt's expanded application of the legend. Eissfeldt, like Gressmann, it seems, did not restrict the legend to a post-exilic setting and consequently could see it, along with the saga, as an important classification for prophetical stories. Eissfeldt even used the term 'prophetic legend' as an apparent sub-division.[4] He viewed Samuel, Elijah, Elisha and Isaiah as 'the classical characters of the

1 *Introduction*, p. 11.
2 *Op. cit.*, p. 294.
3 *Op. cit.*, pp. 38-56. Eissfeldt *did* broaden his use of legend to include stories about holy places as well as persons, but this was not a factor in relation to the Elisha stories.
4 *Op. cit.*, pp. 42-47. Eissfeldt placed prophetic legends alongside cult-legends and martyr-legends.

prophetic legend'.¹ Eissfeldt was quick to point out that the narratives surrounding these figures were quite varied in character. Some he connected with the 'exalted feeling' of the hero saga, whereas others he associated with the historical narrative because of their linkage to political events. Consequently, when it came to the three main stories of 2 Kings 5–7, Eissfeldt assigned 6.8-23 and 6.24–7.20 to the category of historical narrative, acknowledging their possession of legendary elements.² Eissfeldt reasoned that in these cases the political activity of Elisha took precedence. On the other hand, Eissfeldt classified 2 Kings 5 as a legend, but one which approached, in his opinion, the historical narrative.³

In summary, it is clear that Eissfeldt followed the basic system and categories developed by Gunkel, even while he applied these types differently and with more fluidity. We can see how the original vagueness of Gunkel's categories together with the loss of his developmental distinctions made legend and historical narrative as important as saga in classifying the prophetical stories. The classification 'prophetic legend' was especially significant, for it was to become an especially prominent option for later scholars in treating the Elisha stories.

The next major introduction to reflect Gunkel's approach to the classification of prophetical stories was produced by the Danish Old Testament scholar Aage Bentzen.⁴ Bentzen offered a comprehensive typology of biblical literature which followed the basic categories set forth by Gunkel and extended by Eissfeldt.⁵

The general remarks of Bentzen on literary classification indicate a certain appreciation for fluidity between categories,

---

1 *Op. cit.*, p. 46.
2 *Op. cit.*, p. 295.
3 *Ibid.*
4 *Introduction to the Old Testament* (2 vols., 6th edn; Copenhagen: G.E.C. Gad, 1961). Bentzen himself provided the English translation (first published in 1948) from the Danish original (first published in 1941).
5 Bentzen's work on narrative classification also interacted with that of the Swedish scholar Gunnar Hylmö, *Gamla Testamentets Litteraturhistoria* (Lund: C.W.K. Gleerup, 1938).

1. Classifying the Elisha Stories 25

the presence of mixed forms, and the possible artificiality of certain distinctions and the like.[1] However, Bentzen's discussion of specific types directly contrasts with Eissfeldt's in stressing qualification above illustration, and here Bentzen seems to have been more inclined toward firm criteria and clear separations between categories.

More interested than Eissfeldt in the historical development of types, Bentzen still moved with Eissfeldt away from a chronological to a topical arrangement. Bentzen regarded attempts to trace the entire history of a literary form as somewhat speculative.[2] Moreover he did not depend, like Gunkel, upon historical criteria to distinguish types. He claimed that not even content but formal and stylistic features alone should be determinative in defining categories.[3] While it is often difficult to see how the formal and stylistic features which Bentzen identified are separable from content,[4] this claim suggests Bentzen's sense of having his own say in literary classification. Still, despite his own touches, Bentzen's work on literary classification as a whole and on that which related to the Elisha stories in particular stands quite close to the work of Gunkel and Eissfeldt.

Like Gunkel, Bentzen gave chief importance to the saga[5] and even stressed Gunkel's subdivision of etiological saga, though going beyond Gunkel in offering his own sub-categories. On the other hand, the hero saga, the broad sub-division within which Gunkel placed the prophetical stories, was redefined by Bentzen as a multi-episodic complex rather than another type, formally.[6]

Alongside the etiological saga, Bentzen's one other sub-division was the legend.[7] Bentzen's definition of legend, which was

---

1 Bentzen, *Introduction*, pp. 232-33.
2 Ibid., pp. 109-11.
3 Ibid., pp. 233-34.
4 This point is also made by Wilcoxen, 'Narrative', p. 86.
5 Bentzen used the English 'legend' to stand for the German *Sage* (or Danish *sagn*). For the German (and Danish) *Legende* he used the English term 'devotional legend'. I, of course, will maintain my previous usages of 'saga' and 'legend' in this discussion.
6 Bentzen, *Introduction*, p. 234.
7 *Op. cit.*, p. 237.

questionable in meeting his own criterion of being only formally based, followed Gunkel's quite closely, stressing religious tendency and an edificatory intention which focused strictly, as against Eissfeldt, upon an exemplary person. Bentzen split this category into several sub-types, namely 'martyr legend', 'priest legend' and 'prophet legend'. Under this last category Bentzen grouped 'a great part of the narratives of Elijah and Elisha'.[1] He resisted placing all of these stories here because of the presence in some of credible contact with prominent historical events. Of these, he specifically mentioned only 1 Kings 18 and 21 and 2 Kings 8 and 9. For such stories Bentzen offered no distinct classification, possibly seeing them as mixed in character or occupying a middle zone between legend and historical writing.[2]

In our glance at Bentzen's work, we have seen once again that despite some modest differences in the range, relative position and application of Gunkel's basic categories, these categories along with Gunkel's terminology and general kinds of argument were carried forward. In the particular case of the classification of the Elisha stories, the three terms of saga, historical narrative, and legend were once again primary in the discussion—a possibility opened up by the same absence of developmental demarcations which was evident in Eissfeldt's presentation and emergent in Gressmann's. Significantly, Bentzen strengthened the relevance of the prophet legend (or prophetic legend, to use Eissfeldt's term) for the Elisha stories, even while subsuming the legend under the saga.

We come now to, arguably, the most influential Old Testament introduction since Eissfeldt's, that of Georg Fohrer in the tenth edition of the work initiated by Ernst Sellin.[3] Like Eissfeldt and Bentzen before him, Fohrer offered a systematically arranged discussion of Old Testament literary forms, but, unlike his predecessors, Fohrer broke his discussion into

---

1 *Ibid.*
2 Bentzen seems to have acknowledged this zone from the other side when he wrote, 'Historiography in Israel develops from the realm of [sagas] and is never completely disengaged from it' (p. 243).
3 *Introduction to the Old Testament* (trans. David E. Green; Nashville and New York: Abingdon, 1965) = *Einleitung in das Alte Testament* (Heidelberg: Quelle & Meyer, 1965).

1. Classifying the Elisha Stories 27

parts which could be placed under the respective canonical rubrics of his introduction: historical and legal books, poetic books, wisdom books and prophetical books. For that part which pertained to the historical and legal books Fohrer independently suggested a further breakdown under rubrics which mostly concerned literary function (requesting and wishing literary types, proclaiming and instructing literary types, reportorial literary types, etc.). Under these new rubrics, however, one meets the familiar literary types seen in the earlier discussions.

Fohrer's discussion resembles Eissfeldt's in being non-defensive about the identity of the types and simply assuming their place and viability with respect to the Old Testament. Seeing a lack of precise boundaries and the presence of fluidity between types posed no problem for Fohrer, who stressed this freely and more explicitly than Eissfeldt.[1] Fohrer observed that 'Israel obviously did not distinguish clearly between the different narrative forms'.[2] Still, Fohrer remained undaunted in his confidence in the value of the basic theoretical distinctions and synchronic definitions characteristic of the foregoing treatments.

While Fohrer showed some interest in a diachronic view of things, he pointed only to general trends in Israel's literary development, such as increasing personalization, nationalization, and theologization among sagas and legends.[3] Whereas Gunkel used historical observations to help mark disjunctions between types, such observations as these by Fohrer only accentuated, if anything, the sense of continuity and fluidity among types. Fohrer, however, kept this discussion to the side where it did not overtly affect his synchronically defined categories.

Concerning that part of Fohrer's discussion which touched directly upon the classification of the Elisha stories, virtually every position taken lined up with views expressed earlier by either Eissfeldt or Bentzen. Fohrer followed Eissfeldt's broader use of legend to refer to stories about holy places and objects as

1 Fohrer, *Introduction*, p. 86.
2 *Op. cit.*, p. 87.
3 *Op. cit.*, p. 93.

well as holy persons.¹ However, Fohrer followed Bentzen in making legend a sub-category of saga. He even echoed Bentzen's further breakdown into priest-, martyr-, and prophet-legends.² And for this last category, he stressed, as did both of his predecessors, the classic figures of Elijah and Elisha.³ His discussion of historical narrative similarly followed the previous treatments.⁴

In his discussion of the Elisha stories, which came later in his *Introduction*, Fohrer likewise found legend and historical narrative, applied in a very non-rigid way, to be the literary types of essential relevance.⁵ The three narratives of particular interest to us (2 Kgs 5; 6.8-23; 6.24–7.20) were placed by Fohrer in a strand of Elisha material which he described as 'rather like historical narrative', yet exhibiting in their individual manifestation 'the features of miracle story, legend, or saga'.⁶

To summarize, we have traced a pronounced continuity in the work of Fohrer, Bentzen, and Eissfeldt as it relates to the classification of the Elisha stories. All three scholars identified these stories with recourse to Gunkel's categories of saga, legend, and historical narrative. We noted that these scholars related, sub-divided and applied these categories more fluidly. This seems to have come naturally from being free from the greater pressure to legitimate these categories and being free from the greater rigidity of Gunkel's developmental scheme. However, the prompting for this more fluid appropriation of Gunkel's types may have come partly from the biblical text itself. Unlike Gunkel, the work of these scholars turned on introducing the biblical text, not the typology. Thus, their shift in vantage probably made them more sensitive to a variability in the biblical text which resisted the simplicity and rigidity of

1 *Op. cit.*, pp. 90-92.
2 *Op. cit.*, pp. 91-92.
3 *Op. cit.*, p. 92.
4 *Op. cit.*, pp. 98-99.
5 *Op. cit.*, p. 234.
6 It seems that 'miracle story', a term not used in Fohrer's introductory discussion of narrative types, is for Fohrer only a descriptive term used in relation to legend. The usage here perhaps accentuates the fluidity of Fohrer's classification.

Gunkel's system. Gunkel himself sensed this variability but explained it completely in terms of a spontaneous stylistic component which decorated the literary conventions rather than as evidence of *other* literary conventions. It is easy to see how taking over Gunkel's types without his romantic interpretation of such variability would have prompted scholars to allow for more variability in and among Gunkel's types. Eissfeldt, Bentzen, and Fohrer did this, and with specific reference to the Elisha stories in 2 Kings 5–7 it meant locating the given stories either between legend and historical narrative or else in a prophetic sub-class of legend.

Whereas Gunkel's classifications were related and applied more flexibly, it was still *his* basic classifications and descriptions which were being observed. With respect to the Elisha stories, the work of Eissfeldt, Bentzen, and Fohrer stands in obvious continuity with and dependence upon the work of Gunkel.

Further evidence of the sustained impact of Gunkel's work on narrative classification is, of course, legion, but perhaps especially telling is the testimony of two very influential guides to Old Testament form criticism—the first, a fairly technical work by Klaus Koch;[1] the other, a more general introduction by Gene M. Tucker.[2] Both scholars emphasized the unsurpassed place and dominating role of Gunkel's work. In the words of Tucker,

> The definitions of the major narrative genres as established by Gunkel more than sixty years ago remain the basis for most general introductions and commentaries on the narrative books of the Old Testament.[3]

Koch spoke similarly of Gunkel's work in his introductory comments.[4]

Both Koch and Tucker agreed also in making legend the

---

1 *The Growth of the Biblical Tradition: The Form Critical Method* (trans. S.M. Cupitt; New York: Charles Scribner's Sons, 1969). The original German edition appeared in 1964 under the title *Was ist Formgeschichte?*
2 *Form Criticism of the Old Testament* (Philadelphia: Fortress, 1971).
3 *Op. cit.*, p. 26.
4 *Growth*, p. x.

primary category for understanding the prophetical stories. This shift, seen first in Gressmann, and then in Eissfeldt, Bentzen and Fohrer, to expand the application of legend to prophetical stories as Gunkel's evolutionary tendencies were given up, was here rather pronounced. Quite flatly in Koch's discussion, narratives about prophets are prophetic legends.[1] Tucker reflected this same assumption in his discussion of legend.[2] While these scholars were not oblivious of finer qualifications related to the complexity, fluidity, and overlap between types,[3] their position was rather clear-cut when it came to classification of the prophetical stories. It is rather easy to see how anyone following their specific guidance would relate the stories of Elisha first of all to legend. In fact, Tucker twice referred explicitly to the Elisha stories of 2 Kings 5–7 as prime examples of legend in the Old Testament.[4]

In terms of our study, these discussions of Koch and Tucker are important because they reflect more than isolated opinion. As guides to Old Testament form criticism, they are, to some extent, representative and pace-setting scholarly statements on these matters.

Alongside the authoritative sources through which we have traced the direct influence of Gunkel's form-critical work on Old Testament narratives as it relates to the classification of the Elisha stories, there stands a tradition of biblical commentaries which reflects this influence as surely, if not as explicitly. The relevant commentaries are important for showing both the transmission of form-critical assumptions and the fact that they impacted on the actual interpretation of these stories. Rather than attempting to sort through the details of individual commentaries, our effort to trace a trajectory of scholarship is better served by pointing to some general patterns.

In the scholarly commentaries since Gunkel nothing

---

1 *Op. cit.*, p. 197.
2 *Form Criticism*, pp. 38-41.
3 Tucker noted the difficulty of demarcating legend and saga (p. 38) and of establishing sub-classes (pp. 32-34), while Koch developed certain additional criteria for sagas and some additional sub-classes (pp. 148-55).
4 *Form Criticism*, pp. 38-39.

1. Classifying the Elisha Stories   31

appears more often in the classification of the Elisha stories than their association with legend. Not only is the category of legend used often to classify this or that particular story, but it is repeatedly seen to represent a large amount, if not most, of the material constituting the Elisha cycle.[1] Admittedly there are some complicating factors in reading this evidence. First, narrative classifications in commentaries mostly come as background comment rather than as the object of the inquiry. Thus, precision and elaboration in the specific terms of, and with direct reference to, the more intentional form-critical studies which we have seen is generally lacking. Similarly, it is not always clear to what extent a reference to the term 'legend' is meant in a technical way. Indeed, in English there is a popular usage of 'legend' which includes any non-historical story handed down by tradition.[2] On the other hand, it is difficult to see how scholarly commentators could have been using such terminology and concepts totally free of the associations which, as we saw, were dominant in the standard reference works of Old Testament scholarship. In some cases, a commentator's consistency with technical usage is clear, such as when the identification of Elisha stories as legends is illustrated by explicit comparison to medieval legends of the saints or when the term 'hagiology' is used.[3] The presence of such descriptions, even where the term 'legend' alternates with or is totally replaced by other designations, such as 'miracle narrative' or 'wonder story',[4] suggests that the category of legend,

---

1 Among the authors of commentaries which give prominence to legend in classifying the Elisha stories are Norman H. Snaith (1954), John Gray (1964), Peter F. Ellis (1968), P. Fannon (1969), John Robinson (1976), and Martin Rehm (1982).
2 *Webster's Third New International Dictionary* (rev. edn, 1969), s.v. 'legend'.
3 See Peter F. Ellis, '1–2 Kings', in *Jerome Biblical Commentary* (ed. Raymond E. Brown *et al.*; Englewood Cliffs, NJ: Prentice-Hall, 1968), I, p. 198; and John Gray, *I & II Kings: A Commentary* (2nd edn; Philadelphia: Westminster, 1964), p. 29.
4 See Stephen Szikszai, 'Kings, I and II', *IDB*, vol. III (ed. George A. Buttrick; Nashville: Abingdon, 1962), p. 32; Norman H. Snaith, 'The First and Second Book of Kings: Introduction and Exegesis', *The Interpreter's Bible* (ed. George A. Buttrick; Nashville: Abingdon, 1954), III, p. 203.

in something of its technical sense, is still in view. Such opting for some term other than 'legend' might involve trying to avoid the popular deprecations so often associated with this term.[1]

Often alongside legend, a second category, which is regularly seen by commentators to be represented in the Elisha stories, is the category of historical narrative.[2] Any significant discontinuities here with the form-critical discussion are scarcely noticeable, despite the variety of terms used, since 'archives', 'records', 'reports' and 'political narratives'[3] are all terms identifiable with the category or sub-categories of historical narrative as established by the scholars following in Gunkel's train. Where historical narrative and legend are seen to be the two chief types represented in the Elisha stories, the stories of 2 Kings 5–7 are identified with legend most of the time or else with a qualified designation standing somewhere between these two types.[4]

A prominent interpretational emphasis emerges in this tradition of commentaries which sees legend as the major classification of the Elisha stories. The stories are repeatedly identified with the purpose of edifying and magnifying the reputation of the prophet Elisha by showing him in the performance of miraculous exploits.[5] Significantly, this purpose closely resembles that with which Gunkel first identified both hero saga and legend in his foundational work.

We are now ready to summarize the ground we have cov-

1 This reasoning is explicitly admitted by Simon J. DeVries, *I Kings* (Word Biblical Commentary, 12; Waco, TX: Word Books, 1985), p. xxxvii.
2 Among commentators so utilizing this term are Gray, Fannon, Robinson, and Rehm.
3 See Fannon, '1 and 2 Kings', in *A New Catholic Commentary of Holy Scripture* (ed. Reginald C. Fuller and Leonard Johnson; London: Thomas Nelson and Sons, 1969), p. 328; Szikszai, 'Kings', p. 32; Walter Brueggemann, *2 Kings* (Knox Preaching Guides; Atlanta: John Knox, 1982), p. 2; James A. Montgomery and Henry S. Gehman, *A Critical and Exegetical Commentary on the Book of Kings* (International Critical Commentary; Edinburgh: T. & T. Clark, 1951), p. 38.
4 So the commentators listed on p. 31, note 1.
5 For explicit statements to this effect see Snaith, 'Kings', p. 13; Gray, *Kings*, p. 12.

1. Classifying the Elisha Stories 33

ered since Gunkel. Although we have not seen an exhaustive record of the extension of Gunkel's work on narrative classification as it related to the Elisha stories, through our look at major introductions, form-critical guides, and scholarly commentaries we have obtained a fairly good perspective on its general course.

We have seen that Gunkel's work has dominated the classification of the Elisha stories. Gunkel specifically designated the Elisha stories as historical or hero sagas, but his main dominance in the classification of these stories has come by way of the extended application of his other categories of legend and historical narrative. This has involved a greater flexibility in the appropriation of Gunkel's narrative categories, which seems to have followed from at least three causes: (1) the lack of definitive boundaries between these categories in the first place, coupled with less pressure to defend any boundaries, (2) more freedom to merge categories due to an abandonment of Gunkel's developmental distinctions, and (3) perhaps a desire to do greater justice to a variability in the biblical text than a flat application of Gunkel's general categories seemed to allow.[1] In connection with this last point, one senses that this more flexible appropriation of Gunkel's categories did not make an appreciable difference in the way the Elisha stories were viewed. Identifying the Elisha stories with a form of legend or with some qualified designation standing somewhere between legend and historical narrative seems to have involved the same basic emphases that Gunkel was making with his variably expressed designation, namely, historical or hero saga.[2] The Elisha narratives, particularly those we have focused upon in 2 Kings 5–7, have continued to be viewed as stories which attempt to inflate the prophetic reputation of a historically authentic figure by showing him in the performance of miraculous feats.

---

1 Gunkel's romantic option of relegating so much of this variability to individual, spontaneous artistry was one which these scholars, it seems, were not inclined to follow.
2 Perhaps we are seeing here a limitation inherent in the generality and commonality of Gunkel's categories.

Departures from Gunkel's Approach

Challenges against the application of Gunkel's narrative categories to the Elisha stories have been generated at two levels. At the more theoretical level, several scholars have recently contested the legitimacy of the accepted definitions and usages of both saga and legend. It has been argued that Gunkel's use of the term *Sage*, because of its pre-literary sense, 'can no longer be considered adequate for genre identification'.[1] Several have rejected the translation of *Sage* by 'saga', insisting that this latter term must be reserved for translating the Scandinavian 'saga', which has been seen to be unrepresented in the Old Testament,[2] although one scholar has defined it in such a way as to identify it specifically with the story complexes in Genesis.[3] When we turn to the term 'legend', we again find a move toward a more restricted usage which disqualifies all reference to any prophetical narratives. 'Legend' has been narrowed to refer only to those narratives which present 'a virtue embodied in a deed' with an implicit call for imitation.[4] Elijah and Elisha have been explicitly dissociated from such narratives, since their extraordinary deeds have been considered far from imitable.[5]

The foregoing criticisms of the terms saga and legend have registered significant problems with these terms as classifications of the Elisha stories, but little has been offered in the way of an alternative. One senses in this discussion dissatisfaction with Gunkel's nomenclature but general approval of his basic narrative groupings and their identifying features.

More decisive breaks with Gunkel have taken place at a practical level among those finding in the biblical text sufficient reason to forsake Gunkel's categories altogether in favor

---

1 Robert W. Neff, 'Saga', in *Saga, Legend, Tale, Novella, Fable: Narrative Forms in Old Testament Literature* (ed. George W. Coats; JSOTS, 35; Sheffield: JSOT 1985), pp. 17-32.
2 E.g. Scullion, 'Märchen'.
3 Neff, 'Saga', p. 32.
4 See Ronald M. Hals, 'Legend: A Case Study in Old Testament Form Critical Terminology', *CBQ* 34 (1972), p. 172, who depends for this formulation upon André Jolles, *Einfache Formen* (Halle: Max Niemeyer, 1930), pp. 23-61.
5 Hals, 'Legend', p. 175.

1. Classifying the Elisha Stories

of other approaches to classification. It is not our concern here to look into all such departures from Gunkel,[1] but only those specifically involving the Elisha stories. The first person after Gunkel to take an entirely different approach to the classification of the Elisha stories was Otto Plöger in a study of the prophetical narratives of the books of Samuel and Kings.[2] Plöger's expressed purpose was to consider whether these narratives constitute an identifiable genre or set of genres.[3] Since Plöger did not explicitly take note of Gunkel's classification work, it is difficult to believe that he was seeing his work as filling in an insufficiently charted area on Gunkel's map. Plöger seems to have been ignoring Gunkel's deductive approach in an effort to establish genre identifications by beginning with the narratives themselves. He proposed to make his genre determinations by identifying recurrent stylistic-formal elements and content in the given set of narratives.[4] Ironically, the fact that this set of narratives was, at the outset, 'given' seems to have strained against Plöger's inductive intentions. To ask whether the stories which focus upon a prophet comprise a distinct type and then argue their distinctiveness by their focus upon a prophet[5] seems a bit circular. But Plöger seems to have been assuming that more specific literary indicators in addition to a prophet-focus were necessary to qualify these stories as a literary type. Even still, one has to ask how the prior basis for grouping these narratives may have affected Plöger's recognition and interpretation of additional recurrent features. All the other recurrent elements which Plöger perceived were seen to converge on the same purpose, that is, the glorification of the man of

---

1 Important examples are C.A. Keller, 'Die Gefährdung der Ahnfrau. Ein Beitrag zur gattungs- und motivgeschichtlichen Erforschung alttestamentlicher Erzählungen', ZAW 61 (1954), pp. 181-91; Claus Westermann, 'Arten der Erzählung in der Genesis', in his *Forschung am Alten Testament* (Munich: Chr. Kaiser, 1964).
2 *Die Prophetengeschichten der Samuel- und Königsbücher* (Dissertation, Greifswald, 1937).
3 *Op. cit.*, p. 5.
4 *Op. cit.*, p. 38.
5 *Ibid.*

God.[1] It is not that a separate look at each one of these narratives is incapable of revealing this constant purpose, but it is the case that a look at these narratives which begins with and flows from a view to their focus upon a prophet is predisposed toward seeing this constant purpose. And in seeing *this particular* purpose, one is struck by how near to Gunkel's emphasis Plöger came. This only raises further reservations as to how inductive Plöger's study really was.

Plöger's study identified two distinct genres of prophetical narrative, namely, prophet-word stories ('Prophetenwort'-Geschichten) and prophet-deed stories ('Prophetentat'-Geschichten).[2] He based these identifications upon fixed patterns of presentation which he discerned for each group. In the prophet-word stories, the word, directed always to the king, recounted the gracious action of God, the falling away of the people, and a divine statement of either promise or threat designed to keep Israel from remaining outside the gracious will of God. Plöger drew attention to the first-person form of this word, its introductory formula, 'thus says Yahweh', and its patterns of introducing the promise or threat with 'behold'.[3] With this scheme Plöger was claiming to identify a narrative type, but it is difficult to see how it pointed to anything more than a pattern for the prophetic word itself, especially in light of the similar insights of later form-critical studies on prophetic speech.[4]

For prophet-deed stories, in which category he placed the stories of 2 Kings 5–7, Plöger recognized a somewhat less-developed scheme: a miraculous deed is preceded by an appeal to the prophet and in some cases a statement which builds suspense; the miracle is then brought about by a word, prayer, or gesture of the prophet and is concluded by a short notice on

1 *Op. cit.*, pp. 24, 65.
2 *Op. cit.*, pp. 39-40. Narratives of the latter genre were also called wonder stories (*Wundergeschichten*, p. 50).
3 *Op. cit.*, p. 64.
4 Werner Reiser, 'Eschatologische Gottessprüche in den Elisa-Legenden', *Theologische Zeitschrift* 9 (1953), pp. 321-38; Claus Westermann, *Basic Forms of Prophetic Speech* (trans. Hugh C. White; Philadelphia: Westminster, 1967); Daniel Kister, 'Prophetic Forms in Samuel and Kings', *Science et Esprit* 22 (1970), pp. 241-60.

1. Classifying the Elisha Stories 37

the result.¹ The question raised against Plöger's other genre identification seems to apply here as well. Has Plöger found the scheme for a prophet-deed story or only the scheme for a prophetic deed?² In either case the more fundamental problem remains: nothing in either of Plöger's schemes shows why glorification of the prophet must have been the controlling purpose. Yet Plöger proceeded as if there could be no other purpose for recording a prophet's words or deeds.

An entirely different controlling purpose for the Elisha stories was argued by Leah Bronner, the next scholar to break ranks with Gunkel.³ Bronner contended that these narratives were not composed 'in order to heighten the esteem' of Elisha, but rather they were written 'as deliberate polemics against Canaanite mythology'.⁴ It seems improper to call this a form-critical classification since it has little to do with literary form in the strict sense. However, it certainly constituted a classification that stood in the place of the more formally based classifications which had been put forward.

To make her case, Bronner began not with internal features of the text but with external factors from the context. She developed the point that during the time of Elijah and Elisha no historical factor was more pronounced than Yahwism's encounter with Baal worship.⁵ Next she surveyed the picture of Canaanite mythology opened up by the Ugaritic texts, unearthed at Ras Shamra from 1929 onwards. She went on to specify and illustrate important motifs in Ugaritic literature which involved various aspects of Baal's activity and dominion, and she then pointed to the occurrence of these motifs in the stories of Elijah and Elisha.⁶ Since Baal-associated motifs of rain, fire, oil and corn, healing, resurrection, etc. were identified in connection with Yahweh in the Elijah and Elisha stories, Bronner took them as evidence of 'polemical paral-

---

1 *Die Prophetengeschichten*, p. 64.
2 Cf. the study of Jan Heller, 'Drei Wundertaten Elisas', *Communio Viatorum* 2 (1959), pp. 83-85.
3 L. Bronner, *The Stories of Elijah and Elisha as Polemics against Baal Worship* (Leiden: E.J. Brill, 1968).
4 *Op. cit.*, p. 139.
5 *Op. cit.*, pp. 1-34.
6 *Op. cit.*, pp. 35-138.

lelism... intentionally aimed to undermine the authority and influence of Baal'.[1] As Bronner summarized it,

> the wonder tales connected with the name of Elisha as the giver of children, healer of the ailing, reviver of the dead, controller of the sources of rain and water, are all aimed to act as a foil against the claim made by pagan mythology that Baal lorded over these elements in the universe.[2]

Concerning the three stories of main concern to us, Bronner noted the 'polemical parallelism' of each. She linked the healing of Naaman in 2 Kings 5 to the concept, found in Ugaritic literature, of physical recovery brought about by the gods. She noted the Israelite king's exasperated question upon receiving Naaman's letter ('Am I God to kill and make alive?') as an instantiation of this concept as well as an allusion to the power to resurrect, also attributed to Baal in Ugaritic mythology.[3] For the story of Elisha's ambush at Dothan (6.8-23), Bronner saw the Lord's horses and chariots of fire in the light of Baal's control of fire and lightning in Canaanite belief.[4] In the case of the story of the Aramean siege of Samaria (6.24–7.20), Bronner pointed to the skeptical question of the king's attendant regarding the prediction of plenteous food on the morrow: 'If the Lord made windows in heaven, how could this thing be?' She saw this as a direct reference to the windows of Baal's house which refer in Ugaritic literature to the rain-producing clouds of Baal.[5]

One wonders how well the motif pointed to in this last biblical story served as a polemic against Baal, since Yahweh emphatically did not save the day through 'windows in heaven' but only by despoiling the fruits of others. There is some doubt that the polemical connections made by Bronner are always intended by the biblical story. And even where her connections seem likely, should we assume that there could not have been other intended connections which would respect but relativize the polemical significance? For example,

1 *Op. cit.*, p. 138.
2 *Op. cit.*, p. 140.
3 *Op. cit.*, pp. 104-105.
4 *Op. cit.*, p. 64.
5 *Op. cit.*, p. 73.

1. Classifying the Elisha Stories 39

while the reference to 'windows in heaven' could have reminded an Israelite listener of Baal's clouds, it even more readily brought to mind the memory of manna raining from heaven in the wilderness (Exod. 16.4).

Bronner's study makes a strong case for the viability of historical-contextual considerations in apprehending what a text is about. However, there is good reason to think that Bronner, like Plöger, mistook the part for the whole. I am referring to more here than the point I just made about Bronner's assumption that the polemical potential of the given motifs must have represented their entire function. I am also referring to Bronner's assumption that identifying a motif is a basis for classifying an entire story. Whereas Bronner claimed in her conclusion to have presented 'a close study of the stories of Elijah and Elisha',[1] she actually offered no more than a survey of the corpus which looked only for occurrences of the specified motifs. Bronner ignored the possibility that the motifs she identified could be anything other than the controlling motifs of the respective stories. By pointing to polemically potent motifs Bronner assumes she was apprehending the entire agenda of the respective stories. To establish this would take what Bronner claimed but failed to give—a close study of the stories themselves.

Soon after Bronner's study, Alexander Rofé argued the need for a new approach to the classification of the prophetical stories precisely on the ground that justice had not been done to the specific content of the individual stories.[2] Rofé set his approach in direct contrast to Gunkel's.

> It has become apparent to me that attempts to classify the prophetical stories will result in the conclusion that such classification cannot be made with the criteria set forth by Gunkel's form criticism.[3]

And again,

---

1 *Op. cit.*, p. 139.
2 Rofé, 'The Classification of the Prophetical Stories', *JBL* 89 (1970), pp. 427-40; 'Classes in the Prophetical Stories: Didactic Legenda and Parable', *VTS* 26 (1974), pp. 143-64; 'The Story of Micaiah ben Imlah and the Question of the Genres of the Prophetical Stories' (Hebrew), in *Reflections on the Bible*, II (Tel Aviv: Don, 1976), pp. 233-44.
3 Rofé, 'Classification', p. 427.

the proper classification of the prophetical stories will not be achieved along the usual lines of form criticism but rather through a study of the content of each narrative based upon the search for the creative activity inherent in the story.[1]

Rofé itemized form criticism's inadequacies in classifying the prophetical stories.[2] First, he pointed to the dominant assumption in form criticism that essential forms consist in the short units which go back to a presumed oral stage. He felt that the longer compositions one meets in the prophetical stories do not accommodate this assumption. Second, Rofé contended that form criticism's focus upon life-setting had little value for the prophetical stories, since 'very little can be said about [their setting] besides the obvious statement that most of the stories were created and transmitted by circles of prophetic disciples'.[3] Third, Rofé found stereotyped locutions, upon which form-critical insight depended, lacking as constitutive elements in the prophetical stories.[4] These considerations brought Rofé to the conclusion that study of the content of each narrative was the only avenue left open for fruitful pursuit of the classification of the prophetical stories.

Whereas Rofé was emphatic about the need to approach classification of the prophetical stories along lines totally different from those stemming from Gunkel, his own approach was continuous with that approach in two significant respects. First, he connected classification to the marking of developmental relationship between types. His sense of literary development did not show the unilinear, evolutionary tendencies of Gunkel, but he was similarly conscious of establishing literary types in terms of their historical relations to one another.[5] The second facet of Rofé's continuity with the approach he was questioning was related to the first. Rofé saw the legend, defined along the standard lines of edification, as the fundamental class of prophetical story from which others had

---

1 Rofé, 'Classes', p. 143.
2 Rofé, 'Classification', pp. 427-29.
3 Rofé, 'Classification', p. 427.
4 *Ibid*. Rofé ignored the work of Plöger in making this judgment.
5 *Op. cit.*, p. 428.

evolved.¹

The two preceding assumptions are decisive for understanding what Rofé really had in mind when he spoke of the need to study the 'content of each narrative'² or 'the individuality of the literary creation'³ or when he called for 'a close reading of the work itself... in line with that trend in literary criticism which insists upon the uniqueness and singularity of each literary creation'.⁴ Rofé was not intending a coherent literary study of each narrative which attended to all of the literary elements of a given narrative in their relation to each other. Instead, Rofé intended a search of each narrative for a specified set of literary elements by which comparison could be made with the plain legend or, as he called it, the simple *legendum*. Such comparison was expected to reveal the degrees and patterns of literary creativity by which class distinctions could then be made.⁵

In his second article Rofé itemized the literary elements with which his content study was concerned.⁶ Rofé pointed first to the perspective of the story, a broadly defined feature which included the level of literary sophistication and the story's chief concern. The second element concerned the way the prophet was depicted, for example, in terms of veneration, biographical information, etc. The final element Rofé mentioned was the place and significance given to the performance of a miracle in the story.

By looking at the treatment of these elements in particular stories against the background of the simple legend, Rofé felt one could identify several classes of prophetical story beyond the simple *legendum*. His own identifications included (1) the elaborated *legendum*, which embroiders a veneration episode with artistic embellishments of character and plot, (2) the vita, which moves away from simple veneration to interest in the

---

1 *Op. cit.*, pp. 429-35.
2 Rofé, 'Classes', p. 143.
3 *Op. cit.*, p. 145.
4 Rofé, 'Classification', p. 429.
5 *Op. cit.*, p. 430. See Rofé's summary comment on p. 440, in which he describes his method as 'tracing back the creative activity which expanded the original form of a folk tale'.
6 Rofé, 'Classes', pp. 143-45.

beginning and end of the prophet's life,[1] (3) the didactic *legendum*, which recounts a wondrous event in a stereotypical way so as to exalt not the prophet but a moral principle or religious truth, and (4) the parable, which instead of fashioning a religious lesson from a wondrous event, fashions a wondrous event from a religious truth.[2] Rofé indicated that in the future other classes might be delineated along these lines.[3]

Of the three Elisha stories of particular concern to us, only 2 Kings 5 was explicitly classified by Rofé, and it was his prime example of didactic *legenda*.[4] The three literary elements specified earlier figured prominently in Rofé's analysis here. Rofé pointed to the way in which miracle was deflated as the main event by being anticipated from the beginning of the story (v.2), thereby allowing it to point to something beyond itself. As regards the portrayal of the prophet, Rofé contrasted Elisha's refusal to utilize magical procedures (v.11) and to receive a gift (v.16) with the acceptance of these as normal prophetic practices in the simple *legendum* (see 2 Kgs 4.42; 6.6). Rofé saw these variations in the depiction of the miracle and the prophet as serving the third constitutive element— the distinct perspective of the story. This he described in terms of the concern to stress several religious truths, including the oneness of God (v.15), the repudiation of magic (v.11), the condemnation of deceit, greed, and theft (v.26), the conversion of the Gentiles (v.19), and the prophetic endowment (v.8) and holiness (v.17) of the land of Israel.

It seems likely that Rofé would also want to classify 2 Kgs 6.8-23 and 6.24–7.20 as didactic *legenda*, since both of these stories move past the miracle to highlight a truth that points beyond both the miracle and the prophet.

Rofé made a compelling case for the use of content study in classifying prophetical stories. He pointed to literary dynamics which showed the impossibility of some of the previous classi-

---

1 Rofé, 'Classification', pp. 433-40.
2 Rofé, 'Classes', pp. 145-64.
3 Rofé alluded to several such categories: biography, historiography, martyrology ('Classification', p. 440), and *exempla* ('Classes', p. 154). For further mention of these see also his more recent article in *Reflections on the Bible*.
4 Rofé, 'Classes', pp. 145-48.

1. *Classifying the Elisha Stories*

fications. By focusing upon variations in the presentation of the miracle and prophet, Rofé offered significant criteria for moving toward the main concern and primary drive of the story, so fundamental to its proper classification.

Still there are aspects of Rofé's classification which seem to hinder perception of the primary drive of the story. To begin with a small matter, but one of import to the Elisha stories we are addressing, the term didactic *legendum* appears to be self-conflicting. Rofé defined the simple *legendum* in terms of veneration of the prophet. One would expect the term didactic *legendum* to indicate continuity with this, but Rofé's definition stressed that something *besides* the prophet was being stressed here. The term itself pulls *against* that toward which Rofé was pointing. This counter-pull in Rofé's terminology here may be symptomatic of a deeper impediment affecting his entire method. Using the simple *legendum* as *the* standard of comparison may have been helpful in revealing that certain prophetical stories are something more than *legenda*, but seeing those prophetical stories only in reference to the *legenda* in the way Rofé did may have hindered full perception of what that 'something more' actually is. In other words, going to a story looking for a certain set of elements with a view toward comparison with the simple *legendum* preconditioned Rofé toward seeing the drive of the story in terms of a conscious response to the simple *legendum* and kept him from first seeing how *all* the story's elements might have been integrated and interrelated with each other around some other controlling drive. In short, elements of content were related to an outside standard before their internal relations to one another had been sufficiently analyzed. Such content study lacks adequate attention to literary structure, which is crucial for determining what is central and what is not.[1]

The foregoing criticism can be illustrated with reference to Rofé's treatment of the Naaman story. Rofé saw the didactic drive of the story manifesting itself in terms of a variety of doctrines that stand forth at various points of the narrative. In contrasting this didactic interest with the veneration interest

---

1 See the helpful comments of Burke O. Long, '2 Kings III and Genres of Prophetic Narrative', *VT* 23 (1973), p. 338.

of the simple *legenda* Rofé bypassed the possibility that these various doctrines had been consciously and artistically united in the interest of a single coherent lesson.[1] This left Rofé to assume that the governing impulse of the story is to be found not so much in the content of the teaching as in the desire to teach *per se*, so as to transcend the banality of the miracle.[2]

Overall the continuity between Gunkel and the narrative study of Rofé is significant.[3] Both scholars envisioned a system of narrative classes which were developmentally related to one another. Both were sensitive to literary creativity and individual artistry in the specific content of narratives. Whereas Gunkel viewed such specific content with a romanticism which removed it from the search for other classifications, Rofé believed that study of specific content was capable of disclosing patterns which justified further classifications. In light of the criticisms which have been made, even here Rofé may have been carrying over a limitation in Gunkel's approach, namely letting his perception of the developmental relations between types of texts limit his perception of what was going on within texts.

If Rofé's work suffered from some limitations, his argument for the fruitfulness of focusing upon specific literary content marked a dramatic step forward in facilitating proper understanding and classification of the prophetical stories and the Elisha stories in particular.

Soon after Rofé first introduced his approach, Burke O.

---

1 Rofé even argued *against* the possibility of any such coherence when, in comparing the Naaman story with the Shunammite story, he concluded, 'The antimony of art and doctrine could not be better epitomized' ('Classes', p. 147). That there is in fact a striking coherence in what the story teaches has been shown by Robert L. Cohn, 'Form and Perspective in 2 Kings V', *VT* 31 (1983), pp. 171-84, and will be further demonstrated in the next chapter.
2 Rofé spoke as if the primary drive for writing was to establish the literary genre! Emphasizing the repudiation of miracle as a major agenda for didactic *legenda*, Rofé said concerning one didactic *legendum* that its author was 'dissatisfied with the gross nature of his source [and] expanded it' ('Classes', p. 151).
3 The recent commentary of Gwilym H. Jones, *1 and 2 Kings* (2 vols.; New Century Bible; Grand Rapids: Eerdmans, 1984), views Rofé's proposals with favor but treats them as mere extensions of Gunkel's classification (vol. 1, p. 69).

1. Classifying the Elisha Stories

Long called for still another approach to the classification of the prophetical stories which took issue with all previous views, including Rofé's.[1] Like Rofé, Long sought 'more precise ways of describing narrative genres as they actually appear in the Old Testament',[2] but he felt that content alone did not provide an adequate basis for establishing genres. In line with the criticisms against Rofé considered above, Long felt that greater attention to narrative structure was necessary to determine 'what is essential content and what is not'.[3] Identifying the essential structure of a narrative suggested to Long a new and adequate basis for determining narrative types.

To get at the essential structure of narrative, Long felt it expedient to utilize Claus Westermann's insight that narrative is constituted by the posing and resolution of dramatic tension in a clearly bounded prose narration.[4] Long sought to plot the structure of narrative precisely in terms of the introduction, the apex, and the denouement of tension.

Long selected the Elisha story in 2 Kings 3 as a test case for his approach.[5] He illustrated the narrative's construction around the heightening and easing of dramatic tension. In this case the tension concerns a shortage of water and an impending military defeat which give way after an oracle of the prophet to a miraculous deliverance in fulfillment of the prophet's words. Long drew attention to the audience with the prophet as the crucial point on which the whole narrative turns. With this in view, Long posited a formal structure, which he called the 'prophetic inquiry schema', outlining it in the following way:

I. Setting and preparation for inquiry
II. Audience with prophet
    a. request for oracle

---

1 Long, 'II Kings 3: An Oracular Fulfillment Narrative', *Society of Biblical Literature Seminar Papers 1971* (Missoula: Scholars Press, 1971), I, pp. 183-205; this article was revised and expanded into '2 Kings III and Genres of Prophetic Narrative', *VT* 23 (1973), pp. 337-48.
2 *Op. cit.*, p. 338.
3 *Ibid*.
4 Westermann, 'Arten der Erzählung in der Genesis', p. 33.
5 Long, 'Oracular Fulfillment Narrative', pp. 184-99.

b. delivery of oracle
III. Fulfillment of oracle[1]

Long pointed to other narratives wherein he found this same schema.[2] Confident that he had identified a typical structure, Long was ready to take the next step to identify a distinct genre. He argued that since the prophetic inquiry schema embodied the theme or function of actualization of prophetic prediction, there was justification for the genre identification of 'oracular fulfillment narrative' for any narrative so *defined* by that theme.[3]

As if constrained by form-critical procedure, Long suggested a *Sitz im Leben* for the oracular fulfillment narrative in the teaching activity of prophetic groups.[4] He stressed the function of this genre to make a theological point, contrasting it with stories about a prophet's mighty acts, which are aimed instead, Long thought, toward 'venerating the holy man and his exclusive, awe-inspiring power'.[5]

At this time, Long did not point toward any other genre identifications for Old Testament narratives or prophetical stories, and he did not explicitly deal with the Elisha stories under review here, but he clearly implied that his method of extrapolating narrative genre through isolating typical structure was *the* way forward in identifying other narrative genres.

Long himself did not pursue further work along these lines. In fact, there followed two additional phases in Long's work on narrative, as we shall see, both of which took other methodological directions. If this bears indirectly upon the merit and promise of Long's view to establish narrative genres on the basis of typical structure, Robert C. Culley's studies of struc-

1 *Op. cit.*, pp. 192-93.
2 *Op. cit.*, p. 193.
3 *Op. cit.*, p. 199. 1 Kgs 17.8-16; 2 Kgs 2.19-20; 4.42-44 and 8.7-15 were identified as belonging to this genre. In 'Genres', p. 347, Long switched to the term 'oracle-actualization narrative'.
4 Long, 'Oracular Fulfillment Narrative', p. 199.
5 *Ibid*. We shall see later how that Long, in a second phase of study, changed his mind about this interpretation of the aim of these miracle stories. See Long, 'The Social Setting for Prophetic Miracle Stories', *Semeia* 3 (1975), pp. 46-63.

1. Classifying the Elisha Stories 47

ture in biblical narratives[1] have direct bearing upon this question. Culley has recently argued and attempted to demonstrate the value of what he has termed 'structural analysis' of biblical narratives. He has differentiated his approach from structuralism, since the latter involves a philosophical stance toward reality which his work has not assumed.[2] He has admitted that a general familiarity with this approach has influenced him.[3] Culley's identification of structure, like Long's, has focused upon the constitutive movement in narrative from complication to resolution, i.e. plot.[4] Unlike Long, Culley is not sure that this is the definitive feature of narrative but only that it is a useful one for the open-ended exploration of relationships and common patterns among biblical narratives, which Culley believes to be in order at this early stage of research into narrative structure.[5]

Culley freely admits the experimental, almost playful nature of his method at every point.[6] He begins by selecting a group of biblical narratives which share some 'prominent feature', with the idea that they are 'likely to have a similar

---

1 'Structural Analysis: Is it Done with Mirrors?' *Int* 28 (1974), pp. 165-81; 'Themes and Variations in Three Groups of OT Narratives', *Semeia* 3 (1975), pp. 3-13; *Studies in the Structure of Hebrew Narrative* (Semeia Supplements; Philadelphia: Fortress, 1976); 'Punishment Stories in the Legends of the Prophets', in *Orientation by Disorientation: Studies in Literary Criticism and Biblical Literary Criticism* (ed. Richard A. Spencer; Pittsburgh: Pickwick, 1980), pp. 167-81.
2 See 'Mirrors', p. 169.
3 *Studies*, p. 112. In 'Punishment Stories', p. 167, Culley mentions as being particularly influential the work of French structuralist A.J. Greimas (see *Sémantique structurale* [Paris: Larousse, 1966]; *Du sens: Essais sémiotiques* [Paris: Seuil, 1970]) and Russian folklorist Vladimir Propp (see *Morphology of the Folktale* [2nd edn, Austin: University of Texas, 1968]).
4 Culley shows no dependence upon Westermann in his understanding and appreciation of plot, although he finally cites Westermann in 'Punishment Stories', p. 179, as one of the few Old Testament scholars to pay attention to plot.
5 'Punishment Stories', pp. 168-69.
6 For example, Culley describes his work as 'fiddling around with OT narratives' ('Themes and Variations', p. 3) and 'playing it by ear for the time being on the side of method' (*Studies*, p. 111).

structure'.[1] He admits the intuitive nature of this selection,[2] yet defends it against complete arbitrariness. The general coherence of the biblical tradition suggests for Culley the legitimacy of such anticipation of relationships among its narratives.[3] Moreover, Culley begins by using very short stories to establish the essential elements by which comparison can proceed.[4] Although he assigns discrete designations, such as 'miracle stories', 'punishment stories', and 'deception stories', these only represent 'loose groupings rather than strict categories'.[5] He stresses that no genre identifications are being implied by these categories.[6] Furthermore, Culley makes it clear that no genre identifications are being *sought* through his study of these categories. He distinguishes his efforts in this regard from those of Long.[7] As Culley explains it, he approaches narratives at a different level from form criticism 'where the concern is with form and function, that is, patterns in the text influenced by the setting in which the text lived'.[8] Culley wants to explore patterns at more abstract levels through comparison within much broader literary contexts. The difference between Culley and Long could be put this way: whereas Long used narrative structure in order to illuminate narrative classification (genre identification), Culley uses narrative classification (loose groupings) in order to illuminate narrative structure.

Of the three Elisha stories being examined in this study, Culley treats only 2 Kings 5. The Gehazi segment in vv. 20-27 is studied within a group of what he calls 'punishment stories', while the previous part of the chapter, though not examined, is designated as a miracle story.[9] As preliminary categorizations intended to facilitate exploration, these designations

1 'Mirrors', p. 172. The 'prominent feature' by which Culley, in each case, marks off a group of narratives has to do with the nature of their tension-resolving action.
2 'Themes and Variations', p. 10.
3 See 'Mirrors', p. 170.
4 *Op. cit.*, p. 172. See also *Studies*, pp. 72 and 111.
5 'Themes and Variations', p. 4.
6 *Studies*, p. 71.
7 *Op. cit.*, pp. 113-14.
8 *Op. cit.*, pp. 112-13.
9 'Punishment Stories', p. 171.

1. Classifying the Elisha Stories   49

should not be taken as replacements or alternatives to the kinds of classifications we have studied up to this point.

What is significant for our purposes is the way Culley's work on narrative structure raises implications for Long's attempt to use narrative structure to establish genre identifications. As was indicated, Culley no less than Long focuses his study of structure upon the assertion and resolution of narrative tension. Yet Culley differs in recognizing that there are various levels of abstractness by which a narrative's structure can be apprehended or outlined.[1] For Culley the level of abstractness is regulated by the group of stories under examination. In Culley's own words,

> The use of a group of similar narratives provides a means of comparison so that the individual narratives exercise a mutual control on each other in determining the common pattern and also the degree of abstraction in which it should be stated. Thus the patterns of structure found is said to be relative to the group being compared.[2]

Obviously, Long was claiming more for the structure apprehended in his study. The structure he identified was taken to be the definitive structure which revealed the function generating the narrative. However, it is difficult to see the warrant which Long had for this claim. The point can be illustrated by a specific case. Long identified the structure of 2 Kgs 2.19-22 in terms of the pattern: (1) situation/crisis; (2) divine oracle; (3) fulfillment/resolution of crisis.[3] Culley sees this same narrative in terms of the following pattern:

1. A party in a problem situation brings it to the attention of a party with power to provide miraculous help.
2. The helper party responds by taking action on the problem.
3. The miraculous result which removes the problem is indicated.[4]

Culley no less than Long has identified a pattern repeated in

---

1 *Studies*, pp. 69-72.
2 *Studies*, p. 111 (tense changed for stylistic purposes).
3 Long, 'Oracular Fulfillment Narrative', pp. 198-99.
4 *Studies*, p. 94.

other narratives which turns on the assertion and resolution of tension. If Culley's outline were used as the definitive guide to function and genre, it would obviously lead to results different from Long's. But Culley knows that his outline is relative. How could Long know that his is not? We began our discussion of Long by appreciating his insight that narrative structure is important for locating the content which defines and determines the narrative. In locating this content Long felt that the key for unlocking function and genre had been found. Yet as Culley's work on narrative structure has clearly shown, there are different ways of grasping or abstracting such content once it is located. These different ways would lead to contradictory results were they to be taken as definitive guides to function and genre. Thus something more than what Long gave in his opening proposal is needed to establish the mode of abstraction which corresponds to the narrative's essential function.

Almost as if responding to the foregoing criticism, Long followed up the studies just reviewed with a second phase of study which attempted to get at narrative genres from another angle. Whereas Long's earlier studies focused upon internal features of the text, this phase of his work gave priority to context.[1]

Long's first study in this vein directly supported his work on the prophetic inquiry schema. After surveying the practices of divination in ancient Mesopotamia, Long pointed to several formalized patterns by which divinatory activity was carried on and also recorded in Mesopotamian texts. Prominent among these patterns were such elements as formal greeting to the source of help, a formulaic statement on the specific inquiry, and a divinatory response.[2] Long was convinced that this correspondence between divinatory practice and divinatory text in Mesopotamia suggested that the institution of prophetic inquiry in Israel had similarly given rise to the prophetic inquiry schema and its related genre which he had

---

1 Long, 'The Effect of Divination upon Israelite Literature', *JBL* 92 (1973), pp. 489-97; 'The Social Setting for Prophetic Miracle Stories', *Semeia* 3 (1975), pp. 46-63.
2 Long, 'Divination', pp. 492-93.

1. Classifying the Elisha Stories 51

earlier delineated.

Long's argument that the literary structure he had identified corresponds to the structure of a ritual practice seems at first sight to reinforce his assumption that he had identified a literary structure in its constitutive terms, such as are capable of disclosing essential function and thus genre. Yet even if Long's literary schema is rendered less arbitrary by being rooted in a ritual practice, it is still no more capable of disclosing the essential function of a narrative. Otherwise Long would have to defend the unlikely position that there could be no functional difference in the performance of a ritual and in the narrating of it in a story.

A subsequent attempt by Long to approach narratives from the side of context was quite directly concerned with establishing narrative function.[1] Focusing upon 'the miracle stories about the prophets', Long took issue with the assumption which has reigned since Gunkel that the esssential function of these stories consisted in the veneration of the prophet in the eyes of pious followers.[2] Long argued that this social function and life-setting had been imported with the term 'legend', which itself had been colored by the hagiographic model of saint veneration.[3]

Identifying parallels from various cultures, Long observed that miracle stories are frequently found in the role of reinforcing the institution of shamanism in societal contexts where shamanism is in a stage of decline.[4] This suggested to Long that the prophetic miracle stories of the Old Testament similarly sprang from an attempt to reinforce the prophetic institution rather than any desire to venerate an individual prophet. To establish this suggestion, Long pointed to the fact that while there are no biblical references to confirm the existence of any cult of veneration, there is ample biblical witness to the religious skepticism and prophetic conflict which could explain the existence of propaganda for the prophetic institution. In Long's own words,

1 Long, 'Social Setting'.
2 *Op. cit.*, p. 46. Long himself had earlier aligned himself with this assumption; see 'Oracular Fulfillment Narrative', p. 199.
3 Long, 'Social Setting', p. 47.
4 *Op. cit.*, pp. 55-56.

It seems likely that telling and retelling miacle stories about the great prophets of the past would have an immediate purpose in reinforcing—for practitioner and layman alike—an institution greatly stressed by turmoil all around.[1]

In an additional study in which he addressed the full range of ways prophetic authority was legitimated and vindicated in Israel, Long argued that not just the miracle stories but the prophetic power acts themselves functioned to demonstrate prophetic authority.[2] Significantly, Long here stressed the role of these stories and actions in establishing not so much the credibility of the prophetic institution as the credibility of an individual as a prophet. In light of this, one wonders whether Long's view of the function of prophetic miracle stories differs significantly from the view he argued against. Earlier Long had stressed vindication of the institution as opposed to veneration of the individual, but here he saw the function of the miracle stories in terms of vindication of the indivudual as well. The only element of contention left for Long would be the difference between vindication and veneration. Admittedly these concerns are not identical, but on the other hand, Long gave no reason for his assumption that vindication must exclude veneration.

In stressing the concern to legitimize prophetic authority, Long undoubtedly drew attention to a historical factor worthy of consideration in coming to terms with prophetic miracle stories. However, one wonders whether external evidence alone is an adequate basis for establishing this as a primary function of these stories. We note that Long was not entirely indifferent to internal features of the text in this discussion. On the basis of literary considerations he argued that some narratives involving miracles, including those he had earlier identified as oracular fulfillment narratives, should not be

---

1 'Social Setting', p. 58.
2 'Prophetic Authority as Social Reality', in *Canon and Authority: Essays in Old Testament Religion and Theology* (ed. George W. Coats and Burke O. Long; Philadelphia: Fortress, 1977), pp. 3-20. See especially pp. 13-16. This argument has been extended recently by Thomas W. Overholt, 'Seeing is Believing: The Social Setting of Prophetic Acts of Power', *JSOT* 23 (1982), pp. 3-31, who likewise draws upon both biblical and ethnographical evidence.

1. Classifying the Elisha Stories

completely restricted to the given function.¹ On the other hand, the claim that these stories have prophetic authorization as a dominant function was seen by Long to stand in no need of additional warrant from within the text. Long argued this point with specific reference to a portion of the Elisha corpus containing the three stories of specific concern to us: 'The fact that themes of hostility and disbelief are absent in the stories of 2 Kings 2–7 need not count against my suggestion'.² Ironically, the stories in 2 Kgs 6.8-23 and 6.24–7.20 quite plainly *do* feature attitudes of hostility and disbelief toward the prophet. While this fact should have strengthened Long's case, Long's failure to see it raises questions about his method.

Whereas in the first phase of his work Long sought to establish narrative function solely upon the basis of structure, we see that in his second phase he sought to establish narrative function upon the basis of certain external factors alone. With regard to the first effort, we saw from the work of Culley the variables which make structure by itself an insufficient key to function. With regard to the second effort, there may be even more variables which cloud such definitive use of the external factors isolated by Long. There certainly existed other prominent contextual factors besides the need to authenticate prophetic authority which could provide viable explanations of the function of prophetic miracle stories, if we are going on extra-textual evidence alone. We remember Bronner's case for a situation ripe for anti-Baal polemics. Recently still another explanation for the determinative contextual factor behind the Elijah and Elisha stories has been found in the 'fundamental antagonism between the ruling elite... and the more or less subservient peasants, whose interests were supported by Yahwistic religion'.³ In light of the multiple ways of

---

1 'Social Setting', p. 48.
2 *Op. cit.*, p. 57.
3 Robert LaBarbera, 'The Man of War and the Man of God: Social Satire in 2 Kings 6.8–7.20', *CBQ* 46 (1984), pp. 637-51. For essentially the same perspective see also Brueggemann, *2 Kings*, pp. 1-6. These treatments, although they could have implications for classification, do not pursue this issue. The details of these treatments, which involve the Elisha stories under review here, will be taken up in the following chapters.

reading the context behind the prophetical stories, we ask again, can Long's view stand upon external warrants alone? Unlike Long's argument, these other explanations of the function of prophetic stories find literary content to support their contextually oriented argument. In view of this and the fact that Long seems to have ignored internal literary evidence pertinent to his case, it is difficult to put very much reliance upon either his method or his results.

We can now recapitulate our discussion of Long up to this point. In the first phase of his study Long stressed the importance of narrative structure in identifying genre. However, we have seen significant difficulties in establishing narrative function either entirely on the basis of narrative structure, as Long did in his first phase of study, or entirely on the basis of contextual factors, as he did in the second phase. Long's shift in focus to contextual factors might suggest his own second thoughts about depending so completely upon narrative structure. Moreover Long seems to have had second thoughts about depending exclusively upon contextual factors as well. He quickly followed his proposal for the social setting of prophetical miracle stories with two articles which argued upon the basis of anthropological field studies of oral literature that we can no longer be very definite in drawing conclusions about the *Sitz im Leben* of a genre, since a genre can have a multiplicity of settings.[1] Long concluded that any 'substantive sociological historical, theological conclusions, when they depend largely upon reconstructions of an original setting, must be treated with extreme reserve'.[2]

Long's apparent misgivings about his own attempts to establish narrative function led him on to a third phase in his study of biblical narratives. One might have expected Long to have opted for a more eclectic approach to narrative function, depending upon multiple factors, both internal and external. Long did not take this route, but before proceeding with his work, it would be helpful to consider the independent efforts of

1 Long, 'Recent Field Studies in Oral Literature and the Question of *Sitz im Leben*', *Semeia* 5 (1976), pp. 33-49, and 'Recent Field Studies in Oral Literature and Their Bearing on O.T. Criticism', *VT* 26 (1976), pp. 187-98.
2 'Oral Literature and the Question of *Sitz im Leben*', p. 35.

1. Classifying the Elisha Stories

one scholar who did take such a route.

In his book-length study of the Micaiah narrative (1 Kgs 22), Simon J. DeVries developed from a broad range of factors a complete scheme of proposed 'subgenres' for all the prophetic narratives of the Old Testament.[1] Placing his attempt at classification over against the attempts of Plöger, Rofé, and Long,[2] DeVries argued for the primacy of function over content and form in defining genre.[3] Yet recognizing narrative function was seen by DeVries to depend upon considerations of both content and form, and context as well. Content was important for DeVries in that the functional identifications of his subgenres were developed in terms of the narratives' dominant motifs.[4] A certain degree of structural conformity was seen to contribute to these identifications even though any strict structural uniformity was thought by DeVries to be ruled out by the freedom of the prophetic spirit.[5] Considerations of context also informed DeVries's classification in a decisive and pervasive way. Most prominent in DeVries's perception of the context of the prophetic narratives was the factor of prophetic conflict.[6] DeVries, not unlike Long, saw challenges to prophetic authority as a major impetus behind the recounting and recording of stories about prophets. He appreciated a variety in the specific situations generated by this general state of affairs, which corresponded to the variety of sub-genres he identified.[7]

Basing his identification of genres upon this entire range of factors gave DeVries's argument a sense of wholeness found wanting in the other proposals we have reviewed. Yet if his

---

1 S.J. DeVries, *Prophet Against Prophet: The Role of the Micaiah Narrative (I Kings 22) in the Development of Early Prophetic Tradition* (Grand Rapids: Eerdmans, 1978). DeVries's classifications were presented as 'subgenres' because he took the category of 'prophet legend', understood in a non-technical sense, to be the 'general genre' which encompassed all the stories of the prophets (p. 52).
2 *Op. cit.*, pp. 52, 79.
3 *Op. cit.*, pp. 53-56.
4 *Op. cit.*, p. 56.
5 *Op. cit.*, p. 73.
6 *Op. cit.*, pp. 1-2. See also p. viii.
7 *Op. cit.*, p. 53.

considerations seem to be more satisfying in their breadth, they may be less satisfying in their depth. DeVries's functional classifications for all of the prophetical narratives of the canon were covered in one swift and sweeping exposition. Offering a brief description of each type and listing its specific examples, DeVries identified the following eleven subgenres of prophetic narrative: (1) power-demonstration narrative, (2) prophetic call narrative, (3) prophet-legitimation narrative, (4) charismatic designation narrative, (5) historical demonstration narrative, (6) succession oracle narrative, (7) prophet-authorization narrative, (8) regal self-judgment narrative, (9) superseding oracle narrative, (10) instrumental fulfillment narrative, and (11) word-controversy narrative.[1] Two subgenres were seen to have a single example each and several subgenres were broken down into further sub-classifications. Of the narratives central to the present study, the Naaman narrative (2 Kgs 5) was designated as a 'prophetic word story', a type of power-demonstration narrative.[2] Under the prophet-authorization category the story of Elisha's ambush at Dothan (2 Kgs 6.8-23) and the story of the siege of Samaria (2 Kgs 6.24–7.20) were identified with 'supplicatory power stories' and 'word fulfillment stories' respectively.[3]

DeVries pointed out that his classifications were tentative, designed to serve his analysis of the Micaiah narrative, and 'not presented as proven or definitive'.[4] He admitted that further study of each pericope was needed,[5] and yet the role of such further study is rendered somewhat unclear by DeVries's assertion that in the classification of prophet stories 'there is as much art involved as science, as much spiritual

---

1 *Op. cit.*, pp. 53-72.
2 *Op. cit.*, p. 54.
3 *Op. cit.*, p. 55.
4 *Op. cit.*, p. 56. In an earlier study on time references in the Old Testament, DeVries gave some of the same prophetical narratives *other* genre classifications, some of which do not show up in his later scheme. See *Yesterday, Today and Tomorrow* (Grand Rapids: Eerdmans, 1975), pp. 267-69. This inconsistency is something of a problem.
5 *Op. cit.*, p. 53. DeVries indicated that he would be addressing this need in a future book (p. 79).

1. Classifying the Elisha Stories 57

empathy with the intent of the story-teller as cold reason'.[1] Brevard S. Childs recently made a similar point in a discussion of the Elijah narratives:

> It is simply not the case that the more historical and literary knowledge acquired, the better one is able to understand the biblical text... Rather the issue turns on the use of proper discernment.[2]

On the one hand, there is a self-evident soundness in such reasoning which is difficult to deny. On the other hand, such a hermeneutical emphasis tends to give license to premature judgment and then undercut any test of accountability. To check this very tendency, Childs stressed the need to re-test one's interpretations in the light of the integrity of the biblical narrative and in the light of its 'family resemblance' with 'the whole history of God's activity with his people'.[3] Perhaps even more pertinent was Childs's conviction that determining the purpose of a story should come only after, not before, careful study.[4] DeVries, by contrast, not only designated narrative purpose but even formalized it by classification *before* the detailed study, which he now commended as a subsequent step, had been done. Here DeVries differs from Rofé, who insisted that classification be the final phase in narrative study.[5]

In short, DeVries has been helpful in recognizing the hazard of basing classification of the prophetical stories on a set of criteria too narrow to do justice to narrative function. He has energized the discussion by indicating the relevance of a broader range of factors and the need for a fresh approach to the prophetical stories in their light. Still his relatively cursory treatment of the classifications make them less than compelling.

1 *Op. cit.*, p. 56.
2 Childs, 'On Reading the Elijah Narratives', *Int* 34 (1980), pp. 129-30. Another scholar, taking the same sort of hermeneutical stance in a study of the Elisha stories, is Jacques Ellul, *The Politics of God and the Politics of Man* (trans. Geoffrey W. Bromiley; Grand Rapids: Eerdmans, 1972), p. 12.
3 Childs, 'Elijah Narratives', pp. 136-37.
4 *Op. cit.*, p. 131.
5 Rofé, 'Classes', p. 145.

Whereas DeVries confidently established function-based classifications of the prophetical narratives by an inclusive, albeit superficial, look at matters of form, setting and content, Long, as we have seen, depended upon an *ex*clusive, though deeper, study, first of form and then of context, in two phases of narrative study each of which left room for second thoughts. The following comment on the prospect of trustworthy reconstructions of narrative setting shows where Long was left after his second phase of study:

> It may even turn out that reconstructions are fundamentally and inherently misleading simply because too many of the necessary data are unavailable. This may have the effect of turning OT scholars back to the final written text, as the first, and only objective, datum they possess.[1]

This last comment by Long not only put a self-imposed question mark over his second phase of narrative research but it also pointed the way to a third phase of study which he soon took up. Not opting for an inclusive orientation, such as we saw with DeVries, Long was left with the option of giving concentrated focus to narrative content. Thus, in his third phase of study Long shifted his focus away from form criticism's more traditional emphases upon structure and setting to an emphasis upon stylistic features, literary patterns, and artistic devices to be found in a narrative's final written form.

Identifying with the wide and growing interest in applying literary-aesthetic methods to biblical study, Long first advocated this shift as a way 'to keep the form critical method vital'.[2] He felt that the fruits of this newer approach forced upon the form critic the need for 'a broader understanding of the various patterns which might govern a narrative text'.[3]

---

1 Long, 'Studies in Oral Literature and their Bearing on O.T. Criticism', p. 198.
2 Long, 'Some Recent Trends in the Form Criticism of Old Testament Narratives', *Proceedings of the Seventh World Congress of Jewish Studies: Studies in the Bible and the Ancient Near East* (Jerusalem: World Union of Jewish Studies, 1981), pp. 63-72.
3 *Op. cit.*, p. 66. Long acknowledged here the important article of Rolf Knierim, 'Old Testament Form Criticism Reconsidered', *Int* 27 (1973), pp. 463-66.

1. *Classifying the Elisha Stories* 59

Up to this point Long's change of course fell completely in line with Rofé. In light of this, one would have expected Long to have proceeded toward proposing new genre designations based upon such study. However, what he propounded was an analysis which explores the artistry of Hebrew narratives without pressing for *any* specific genre designation.[1] In fact, in his recent form-critical commentary on 1 Kings, Long designated the Elijah stories with recourse to the very general categories associated with Gunkel,[2] rejecting more specific genre designations including his own,[3] on the grounds that giving a narrative more specific classification would unduly restrict its literary uniqueness and richness.[4] Unlike other scholars who had taken up Gunkel's categories, Long did not carry them toward greater specification and more sub-classes but rather toward greater generalization, to the point of stressing their identity as manifestations of the even more general category of 'story', defined simply as a narration moving from tension to resolution.[5] A comment by Long on 1 Kings 18 is representative of his approach:

> In view of the uncertainties and the proliferation of generic designations which emphasize unduly one or another aspect of the material, it seems wisest to retain the more open-ended and descriptive term legend.[6]

---

1 Long, 'Artistry in Hebrew Historical Narrative: Observations on 1–2 Kings', *Proceedings of the Eighth World Congress of Jewish Studies: The Period of the Bible* (Jerusalem: World Union of Jewish Studies, 1982), pp. 29-34; *I Kings with an Introduction to Historical Literature* (Forms of Old Testament Literature, 9; Grand Rapids: Eerdmans, 1984); 'Historical Narrative and the Fictionalizing Imagination', *VT* 35 (1985), pp. 405-16.
2 Traditional definitions of *Sage*, *Legende*, and *Historische Erzählung* appear in Long's glossary: *I Kings*, pp. 243-65.
3 Long, *I Kings*, pp. 181-82, ignored his own earlier case for designating 1 Kgs 17.8-16 as an oracular fulfillment narrative (see his 'Oracular Fulfillment Narrative', pp. 198-99) and explicitly rejected the more specific genre designations of other scholars, including Plöger and Rofé. See also *I Kings*, pp. 186-94.
4 *Op. cit.*, pp. 181-82, 186-94.
5 *Op. cit.*, pp. 261-62. See also p. 181.
6 *Op. cit.*, p. 194.

It is important to remember that Long began his study of Old Testament narratives with a rejection of 'Oberbegriffe such as legend, saga, and the like' in view of the need for 'more precise ways of describing narrative genres as they actually appear in the Old Testament'.[1] Whereas Long at first rejected these traditional classifications because of their generality, we see that he came at last to accept them precisely because of their generality, that is, because they leave plenty of room for the literary-aesthetic exploration of specific content in the same way that they had left plenty of room for Gunkel's romantic interpretations of specific content. Yet given this rationale, the question becomes, why should there even be any genre classifications at all?[2] Why go beyond the all-inclusive classification of 'story'? This question gains force from the fact that as Long repeatedly tried to see narratives in terms of a multiplicity of functions and settings, story was the only category which actually remained essential to his interpretation.[3] It is ironic that someone promoting literary-aesthetic methods as a way to keep form criticism vital would argue for a return to the traditional classifications, which more recent studies, including his own, had rejected as inadequate, and do so in such a way as to evoke the question whether there is even a need for narrative classifications at all.

The force of this last point is brought home by T.R. Hobbs's recent commentary on 2 Kings.[4] Hobbs advocates here a literary-aesthetic approach which explicitly dismisses all genre classification as inconclusive and of marginal significance.[5]

1 Long, 'Genres', p. 338.
2 Gunkel, in seeking to trace the history of Israelite literature, had a reason for establishing categories which Long did not have. See the discussion of Gunkel above.
3 Long, *I Kings*, pp. 183, 187, 195-96.
4 Hobbs, *2 Kings* (Word Biblical Commentary, 13; Waco, TX: Word Books, 1985).
5 *Op. cit.*, p. 17. Two other recent works have approached the Elisha stories in a similar fashion, although their posture toward form-critical classification is more that of relative indifference than direct challenge. See Brueggemann, *2 Kings*, p. 3; Terence E. Fretheim, *Deuteronomic History* (Nashville: Abingdon, 1983), pp. 36, 44. Also fitting here, though with less literary-critical refinement and intentionality, might be Ellul, *Politics of God*; see p. 12.

1. Classifying the Elisha Stories

Hobbs feels that no identification of narrative type is needed to understand a story beyond its mere identification as a story on the basis of its movement from problem to solution.[1] For the Elisha stories he consistently and summarily dismisses the specific genre classifications of Eissfeldt, Rofé, DeVries, and even Long as a hindrance to full and holistic interpretation.[2] A comment by Hobbs on one Elisha story is representative:

> The perpetual danger in the search for common formal features is that the common elements are stressed to the detriment of the individual features. It is precisely in the particulars of a given story that the genius and intent of the writer can be seen.[3]

Hobbs's commentary is significant to us for extending the literary-aesthetic approach taken up by Long into the Elisha materials[4] and also for extending Long's reasoning concerning the need to back away from restricting the literary exploration of biblical narrative with genre classification to its logical conclusion. Long's expressed reasons for returning to the very general genre classifications of Gunkel are not different from Hobbs's reasons for brushing aside *all* genre classifications in favor of the all-inclusive category of story. In fact, one might ask whether Long himself has actually defended any narrative classification other than that of story. Long seems to have offered not so much an argument *for* the traditional categories as an argument *against* everything else. And at the same time, Long has treated the category of story, upon which he has based his identification of the traditional categories, as if

---

1 *Op. cit.*, p. 45.
2 *Op. cit.*, pp. 16-17, 45, 58, 61, 72, 88, 98.
3 *Op. cit.*, p. 45.
4 We should note that while Hobbs's commentary represents the first full-scale coverage of the Elisha material from a literary-aesthetic approach, the studies of Brueggemann, Fretheim and even Ellul mentioned earlier are significant, though more modest, efforts in this vein. Moreover there are several studies prior to Hobbs's which have applied such an approach to more limited portions of the Elisha material, e.g. Kenneth R.R. Gros Louis, 'Elijah and Elisha', *Literary Interpretations of Biblical Narratives* (ed. Gros Louis; Nashville: Abingdon, 1974), pp. 177-90; Jacob Licht, 'Story Telling in the Bible', *Immanuel* 7 (1977), pp. 21-24; Cohn, 'Form and Perspective'; LaBarbera, 'Man of War'.

it were the only classification essential to proper interpretation of the text. In this light, even this final phase of Long's work can be seen to represent something of a departure from Gunkel's way of classifying the prophetical narratives.

The thrust of the work of Hobbs and Long here has been to make sure that genre classification does not inhibit full literary-aesthetic interpretation of the text. This same concern has heavily informed my own critique of classification efforts since Gunkel. In the foregoing discussion I have suggested that in one way or another the classification proposals of Plöger, Bronner, Rofé, Long (in his earlier studies), and DeVries have not done justice to the literary specifics of the narratives. However, what Long has failed to show and what Hobbs has effectively given up on showing is how literary-aesthetic analysis can lead to new and refined judgments on specific genre classification.[1]

The issue at stake here is not genre classification for its own sake but, as all along, the proper interpretation of the text.[2] I agree with Long and Hobbs that the specific genre classifications which have been proposed thus far for the prophetical narratives of Kings have prematurely closed off interpretation, preempting the light of full literary-aesthetic analysis. However, I believe that Long and Hobbs have responded to premature closure with insufficient closure. In pursuing a literary-aesthetic approach which is committed to leaving matters of classification so open, they have themselves stopped short of adequate interpretation. They have set out to explore the unique literary features within each individual text without expecting or noticing how there might be typicalities and outside factors which cohere with these features so as to reveal a quite specific pattern of meaning and function. As I intend to demonstrate in the following chapters, certain narrative designs do not become apparent without striking a better balance between the unique and the typical and between the internal and the external factors of the text than

---

1 A positive view on this prospect emerges from Knierim, 'Form Criticism Reconsidered'.
2 See George W. Coats, 'Genres: Why Should They Be Important for Exegesis?', in *Saga, Legend, Tale*, pp. 7-15, for a strong statement on the importance of genre identification for exegesis.

Long's and Hobbs's reaction to specific genre classification allows them.[1] Without this balance I believe that our escape from proliferation of different genre classifications will only lead to a proliferation of different literary interpretations.

Summary

The essential test for the adequacy of any treatment of the three main Elisha stories of 2 Kings 5–7 rests with how well it can account for all of the features and factors of these narratives. This criterion underlies the foregoing critique of the main proposals relevant to the classification and interpretation of these narratives, beginning with Hermann Gunkel. However, this critique can be fully vindicated, I believe, only in the light of the full examination of these narratives which follows. Before proceeding, it will be helpful to review the ground we have covered.

We began with Gunkel because his influence so dominated subsequent treatment of these Elisha stories. This was true not because of his direct comment on these narratives but because he developed the comprehensive system of narrative classifications which dominated the study of all biblical narrative. Three categories of Gunkel's system became important to subsequent classification of the Elisha stories—historical or hero saga, historical narrative, and legend. Gunkel gave these categories very broad and overlapping definitions which later scholars found problematic. However, such definitions were precisely suited to Gunkel's major agenda of linking categories together to show a developmental scheme. In turn this scheme provided chronological distinctions which helped Gunkel keep these categories apart without recourse to more refined definitions. The generality of Gunkel's categories left much to be said for the specifics of biblical narratives. Gunkel responded to this in terms of a romanticism which interpreted all the literary features that went beyond the broad features constituting his narrative types as products of the free and

---

1 Specific criticisms of Hobbs's treatment of the Elisha stories under review here will be taken up in the following chapters. Long's comment on these stories is forthcoming in his next volume on Kings.

spontaneous artistry of the storyteller. This tilted Gunkel away from seeing any more specific patterns which might have complicated his developmental scheme. Gunkel's broadly defined classifications were thus tied to a developmental approach to narrative types and a romantic approach to narrative content which later scholars left behind, even as they took up his basic categories.

Our look at major introductions, form-critical guides, and biblical commentaries gave clear evidence of the dominance of Gunkel's categories in subsequent treatment of the Elisha stories. The great deal of flexibility we saw in subsequent understanding and appropriation of these categories suggested certain problems with Gunkel's typology in the face of the biblical text. The category of legend became increasingly prominent in identifying the Elisha stories. Still, in all of this, the basic interpretation of the meaning and function of these stories remained essentially unchanged. The stories of 2 Kings 5–7 continued to be seen as narratives designed to edify the prophetic reputation of a historically authentic figure through the recounting of his miraculous exploits.

Otto Plöger was the first to depart from Gunkel's categories in classifying the Elisha stories. Proposing to work upward from the text rather than downward from the typology, Plöger sought fresh classifications based on recurrent patterns of style and content. However, his argument for two discrete narrative types, the prophet word story and the prophet deed story, seems to have pointed up patterns for prophetic words and deeds rather than patterns which define entire narratives. Moreover Plöger seems to have brought to his study the earlier assumption that veneration of the prophet must be the controlling purpose served by narratives which feature a prophet's words or deeds.

Leah Bronner, who made the next attempt to classify the Elisha stories along lines different from Gunkel, identified another controlling purpose for these stories. Giving prime consideration to historical context, Bronner argued that the Elijah and Elisha stories were polemics against Baal worship. While Bronner pointed to motifs in these stories which could have functioned in this way, she did not demonstrate that entire narratives were controlled by this purpose.

1. Classifying the Elisha Stories   65

Alexander Rofé argued that a fresh approach to classification of the prophetic narratives was needed and possible through a close study of the content of each narrative. Rofé's content study demonstrated that certain prophetical narratives were something more than legends, but his assumption that these narratives were governed by the conscious attempt to transcend the simple legend limited what content he looked for and how he interpreted it. This was seen in his treatment of the Naaman narrative, which was his prime example of what he called the didactic *legendum*. Rofé's assumptions led him to locate the drive of this story in the aim to teach *per se* and kept him from seeing how all the didactic elements of the story were deliberately and artistically integrated in the interest of a single coherent lesson. Rofé related elements of content to the external standard of the simple legend before perceiving their internal relations to each other. His content study gave inadequate attention to literary structure.

The next new approach to classifying the Elisha stories came from Burke O. Long, who argued and tried to demonstrate that narrative structure was the key to proper classification. However, Long's attempt to determine genre exclusively upon the basis of structure was seen to have problems in the light of Culley's studies on narrative structure. Since narrative patterns can be apprehended at different levels of abstraction, something more is needed to establish that the structure of a given narrative is being grasped in terms corresponding to constitutive function. Long himself may have had misgivings about such exclusive dependence upon structure, as his pursuit in this vein quickly gave way to a second phase of study which made narrative context the primary focus. Here Long argued that the Elisha stories, instead of being categorized as prophet-edifying legends, should be regarded as apologies for the embattled prophetic institution. Citing ethnographic parallels, Long contended that the contextual evidence for prophetic conflict in Israel was sufficient to establish this purpose for the miracle stories of Elisha in the absence of corroborating evidence from the content of these stories. However, the multiplicity of possible contextual determinants makes such identification of narrative function on contextual grounds alone even more dubious than basing such conclusions solely upon structure, as Long's own subsequent reservations about scholarship's access to narrative *Sitz im Leben* would help to show. Whereas Long's exclusive focus, first upon structure and then upon setting, never gave way to a more eclectic approach to narrative function, which synthesized internal and external evidence, Simon DeVries followed just such an approach to arrive at a completely new and comprehensive set of classifications for all of the prophetical stories of the Old Testament. Drawing upon dominant motifs, structural affinities and contextual factors, DeVries summarily set forth eleven function-based categories of prophetical narratives, with sub-categories for some. Under these categories he placed every prophetical narrative of Samuel and Kings. He designated the Naaman story as a 'power-demonstration narrative' and categorized the other two Elisha stories central to the present study as 'prophet-authorization narratives'. DeVries's scheme of classification remains somewhat doubtful, however, in the absence of detailed study of the individual narratives, and despite (or perhaps because of) his appeal to the priority of 'spiritual empathy with the intent of the storyteller' over 'cold reason'. DeVries showed little awareness of how designating narratives so specifically prior to close analysis can inhibit interpretation.

This latter concern weighed heavily in a third phase of study which Long soon took up. Long embraced the literary-aesthetic interpretation of narrative as a means of revitalizing form-critical study, but then, rather than proceeding to new and refined genre specifications, Long drew back from specific genre classification altogether, reverting explicitly to the general categories of Gunkel and functionally to the ultra-general category of story. T.R. Hobbs, whose recent commentary has treated the entire Elisha cycle from a literary-aesthetic perspective, has advocated an even more explicit departure from classifications more specific than story. There is no doubt that the proliferation of specific narrative classifications has been closed to the manifold internal features which literary-aesthetic analysis has begun to open up. On the other hand, the reaction to specific genre classification by Long and Hobbs leaves them unprepared to perceive certain specific patterns

1. Classifying the Elisha Stories

of meaning and function which are crucial to avoiding a proliferation of different literary-aesthetic interpretations.

This review of research on the classification of the Elisha stories has given us a way to see the past interpretations of our particular stories in the broader context of the scholarly agendas actually generating these interpretations. Through this we have attained a clearer perspective on the methodologies at work in these interpretations and on the points at which they seem to be inadequate. This has been done not in order to make a case for some new, definitive methodology for narrative classification but only to indicate the need for a fresh examination of three particular Elisha stories.

Obviously the following examination of the given stories will proceed along definite methodological lines, which could be taken as having implications for the study of other narratives. However, these lines are not intended to constitute any definitive formula for narrative interpretation, and my own sensibilities make me doubt that anything could. The methodological approach pursued here should seem reasonable in light of the strengths and weaknesses noted in the earlier approaches. I begin with a literary-aesthetic analysis of each of the given narratives, because I have found this to be the most thorough and penetrating avenue into all the internal features and dynamics of narrative texts, and because I think that attending to the internal features of each narrative first helps avoid the tendency we saw to override a text's own inner workings with external considerations. Still I have found it essential to proceed to an examination of contextual matters, viewing context not exclusively nor even primarily as sociological setting, but as inclusive of the more definite relationships each Elisha story has with other Elisha stories and with the historical, political, and religious situation of ninth-century Israel. I have found such study crucial for seeing a narrative's internal dimensions in the proper perspective of meaning and function.

The test of interpretation finally is not the method one uses, since any method can be used badly. The final test of interpretation remains the text itself and how well all of its internal and external aspects and relationships are accounted for and held together in a mutually informing way. If there is little chance of a definitive methodology, there is probably even less chance of a definitive interpretation. Nevertheless the following study is pursued in the confidence of advancing our understanding of the three main narratives of 2 Kings 5–7.

Chapter 2

THE THREE ELISHA STORIES
IN LITERARY-AESTHETIC PERSPECTIVE

Introduction

This chapter will offer a literary-aesthetic analysis of the three Elisha stories found in 2 Kgs 5, 6.8-23, and 6.24–7.20. My term 'literary-aesthetic analysis' refers to a general approach which has now established itself in biblical studies to the point of needing little introduction. Associated with several more formal terms, such as 'rhetorical criticism',[1] 'aesthetic criticism',[2] and even 'literary criticism',[3] the general

---

[1] James Muilenburg, 'Form Criticism and Beyond', *JBL* 88 (1969), pp. 1-18. See also *Rhetorical Criticism: Essays in Honor of James Muilenburg* (ed. Jared J. Jackson and Martin Kessler; Pittsburgh: Pickwick, 1974), and Phyllis Trible, *God and the Rhetoric of Sexuality* (Philadelphia: Fortress, 1978). For a more recent discussion see Martin Kessler, 'A Methodological Setting for Rhetorical Criticism', in *Art and Meaning: Rhetoric in Biblical Literature* (ed. David J.A. Clines, David M. Gunn, and Alan J. Hauser; JSOTS, 19; Sheffield: JSOT, 1982), pp. 1-19.

[2] James L. Crenshaw, *Samson: A Secret Betrayed, A Vow Ignored* (Atlanta: John Knox, 1978). This term is also used by Edward L. Greenstein, 'Biblical Narratology', *Prooftexts* 1 (1981), p. 202.

[3] E.g., Edwin M. Good, review of *Literary Criticism of the Old Testament*, by Norman Habel, in *JBL* 92 (1973), pp. 287-89; David A. Robertson, *The Old Testament and the Literary Critic* (Philadelphia: Fortress, 1977). Most would take 'literary criticism' as the generic term standing over the whole array of literary-oriented approaches, e.g., Trible, *God*, p. 8, who stresses the distinction with source criticism, and, more recently, Rolf Knierim, 'Criticism of Literary Features, Form, Tradition, and Redaction', ch. 4 in *The Hebrew Bible and its Modern Interpreters* (ed. Douglas A. Knight and Gene M. Tucker; Philadelphia: Fortress, 1985; Chico, CA: Scholars, 1985), pp. 123-65, who includes even source criticism in his usage. See

approach in view here is concerned with the stylistic features and literary artistry of biblical texts in their wholeness. Over the past decade, this approach has gained particular distinction in the study of biblical narrative.[1] The kind of study I propose here stands within this general tradition of study, and I mean nothing new and special by the term 'literary-aesthetic analysis'.

While the next chapter will more fully treat the relationship between these Elisha stories, a preliminary comment justifying my treatment of just these three narratives is perhaps in order. A certain set of features distinctly shared by these stories suggests a basic kinship among them. All three stories (1) are set in the context of Aramean warfare against Israel, (2) refer to the current Aramean and Israelite kings without giving them specific identification, and (3) present dramatic miracles which do not constitute the climax of the story but rather point beyond themselves in each case to serve a larger message. The fact that this important set of factors is present only in these three Elisha stories indicates the appropriateness of looking at them alongside one another. The fact that they are already alongside one another in their canonical placement, except for the short 'interruption' of 2 Kgs 6.1-7, may not be entirely irrelevant to the issue; however, I would see such considerations as belonging after rather than before the kind of study I am pursuing here.

Knierim's article for a valuable and recent survey of the approach.
1 Since the mid-seventies there has been a veritable deluge of literary-aesthetic studies on Old Testament narrative too numerous to list. Until recently almost all of this work on Old Testament narrative had concentrated on the exposition of specific examples of literary artistry rather than the apprehension and exposition of general theory. This fact was observed in the 1981 review article of Greenstein, 'Biblical Narratology'. Since this article, however, elaboration of general theory has become a prominent, if not the commanding, focus of Hebrew narrative study through the impact of three important studies: Robert Alter, *The Art of Biblical Narrative* (New York: Basic Books, 1981); Adele Berlin, *Poetics and Interpretation of Biblical Narrative* (Bible and Literature Series; Sheffield: Almond, 1983); Meir Sternberg, *The Poetics of Biblical Narrative: Ideological Literature and the Drama of Reading* (Indiana Literary Biblical Series; Bloomington: Indiana University Press, 1985).

2. The Stories in Literary-Aesthetic Perspective 71

2 Kings 5.1-27

The story of 2 Kings 5 begins with the character profile of an Aramean general, Naaman. He is a man who ranks high not only in position but in respect and honor as well, so that the greatness of his character befits the greatness of his name, which signifies 'pleasantness', or 'charm'.[1] However, after a lengthy description of his laudable characteristics there follows a one-word, participial phrase which presents a stark counterpoint to all we have heard about this 'great man' (איש גדול). Naaman is a leper.[2] The contrast creates narrative tension, and the narrative leaves us suspended at that very point and leaps ahead to introduce a second character.

The Israelite captive girl is introduced into the story almost indirectly (v. 2). Naaman, the subject of the preceding verse, appeared as the very first word, but this little girl makes her entrance as a direct object. This grammatical contrast reflects an actual contrast which exists between them. Naaman is the subject of military conquest, while the captive lass is an object of military conquest. The reader is given a decisive indication that such comparison between these two characters is intended. Naaman is described as 'a great man before his lord'; the Hebrew lass is called 'a little girl, and she was before Naaman's wife'. The preposition לפני conspicuously follows the generic designation of each character. Parallel wording[3] invites juxtaposition of these two figures, and juxtaposition yields a nearly perfect antithesis,[4] an entire series of contrasts:

---

1 See J.M. Ward, 'Naaman', *IDB*, III, p. 490.
2 For a discussion of this disease and related issues see R.K. Harrison, 'Leprosy', *IDB*, III, pp. 111-13.
3 The only difference in wording stems from the fact that 'a little girl' is the direct object of the preceding phrase.
4 Cohn, 'Form and Perspective', p. 174, notes this contrast, pointing to the parallels in wording. Furthermore, Cohn recognizes, as I have done, that the ruler-servant antithesis opens up the literary-aesthetic dynamics of the entire story. Cohn's is the only study published to date which has fully recognized the artistic integration of the story around this antithesis. My own interpretation, which was worked out independently of and even prior to the publication of Cohn's fine study, intersects with Cohn's at many points, corroborating much of what Cohn has recognized. In the footnotes which follow I will note our points of agreement and Cohn's additional

great (גדול) vs small (קטן), Aramean vs Israelite, conqueror vs captive, male vs female, adult vs child, and ruler vs servant. The radical contrast here presented is further highlighted by the anonymity of the little girl. Over against the greatness and supreme importance of Naaman, this Hebrew maid fails to merit a name.[1] She retains her obscurity. However this nameless lass does not remain unimportant for long. She bursts forth from her insignificance with the narrative's first speech (v. 3), words which introduce the possibility of solution for Naaman's problem, words which anticipate the goal toward which the narrative will now move. It is an irony that one so lowly delivers a speech of such profound importance to the story line. Yet it establishes a pattern which will dominate the first movement of the story: help and solution for the great one will be mediated through lowly persons.[2]

In the first three verses the narrative has set the stage. The story is given national dimensions. An uneasy peace exists between Aram and Israel. Marauding bands have been raiding Hebrew territory.[3] Aram is obviously in a position of military superiority. Yet the narrative is careful to include one other background detail. Yahweh stands behind Aram's military success. He is the one responsible for Naaman's victory. This detail, pregnant with implications,[4] establishes at the outset a theological dimension to the story.

We first meet the prophet Elisha in the little girl's speech. The little girl's anticipatory words deserve special note. 'If only my master were before the prophet who is in Samaria', she says, 'then would he cleanse him from his leprosy' (v. 3). For the third time the narrative makes use of the preposition לפני; for the second time it is applied directly to Naaman. Naaman

> insights, as well as the one instance where I am dependent on Cohn's study. I will also note where my insights have intersected with others who have seen only certain pieces of the entire artistic unity of the story.
> 1 This is noted by Ellul, *Politics of God*, p. 31.
> 2 So von Rad, 'Naaman: A Critical Retelling', in *God at Work in Israel* (trans. John H. Marks; Nashville: Abingdon, 1980), p. 48; Ellul, *Politics of God*, p. 30; Hobbs, *2 Kings*, p. 92.
> 3 See Gray, *Kings*, p. 504; Hobbs, *2 Kings*, p. 63.
> 4 Von Rad, 'Naaman', p. 48, draws attention to the great notice such a remark would have attracted in ancient Israel.

2. The Stories in Literary-Aesthetic Perspective 73

is *before* his lord; if only he were *before* the Israelite prophet. In both cases לפני can be understood in a locative sense, meaning 'in the presence of' or literally 'at the face of'.[1] However, this preposition can also be understood in another sense, as is illustrated in v. 2 when applied to the little girl. Here לפני conveys the idea of 'being in the service of' or 'being under the authority of'.[2] I would suggest that when לפני is applied to Naaman (vv. 1, 3) this second meaning is resonating below the surface. The narrative is deliberately employing double entendre, pregnant terminology. The great Naaman, who is under the authority of the king of Aram, will receive his healing if and only if he comes under the authority of God's prophet. The little Hebrew girl, then, is unwittingly pronouncing the condition upon which Naaman's healing will be predicated.[3] In order to experience a transformation of physical condition, Naaman must experience a transformation of allegiance. The leper must become a servant.

Later on in the story we are given unmistakable evidence that this interpretation is the correct one. In v. 14, when Naaman emerges from the muddy waters of Jordan he is compared to נער קטן, properly translated 'a little lad'. However, once again the narrative has employed a word with a second nuance which is associated with servitude; נער can also mean 'servant',[4] as indeed it does in v. 2 (נערה). Is the narrative once again intending for this second meaning to resonate below the surface? The conclusion is irresistible, for נער קטן is the precise verbal echo of נערה קטנה, the designation for the little servant girl (v. 2).[5] Naaman's skin has become as that of 'a little child', but by using נער the narrative is highlighting another change that has taken place. Naaman has become a servant.

We can now understand the significance of the contrast set up between Naaman and the servant girl. She *is* what

---

1 *A Hebrew and English Lexicon of the Old Testament* (ed. Francis Brown, S.R. Driver, and C.A. Briggs; Oxford: Clarendon, 1907), p. 816.
2 *Op. cit..*, p. 817.
3 Cohn, 'Form and Perspective', p. 178, observes this.
4 *Hebrew and English Lexicon*, p. 654.
5 This is noticed by Cohn, 'Form and Perspective', p. 177; Fretheim, *Deuteronomistic History*, pp. 150, 153; Hobbs, *2 Kings*, pp. 60, 65.

Naaman must become, namely, נער קטן. She realizes what Naaman must come to realize, namely, that there is a prophet in Israel (vv. 3, 8). The איש גדול with a problem stands over against the נערה קטנה with a solution. However, a long journey stands between a leper and his cure.

The characters having been introduced, the story begins to move, and one is struck by the swiftness of narrative pace.[1]

Naaman, who does not really become involved in the speaking until after he hears from Elisha's messenger in v. 11, is swept along by the words of others. Yet the Aramean is not entirely passive. His initiative manifests itself in two actions—in the solicitation of the king's letter and in the taking of expensive gifts with him to Israel (v. 5). These represent the Aramean's effort to gain his healing.[2] Naaman's bag of riches and letter from his king represent the chief resources of royalty, namely, wealth and power. In the end, both resources fail. Naaman discovers that his healing will cost something other than money, and he further discovers that he must acknowledge something that the king's letter fails to acknowledge, namely, that there is a prophet in Israel.[3] His display of power succeeds only in terrorizing a nervous king, while his display of wealth succeeds only in enticing a greedy servant. Naaman's efforts are doomed by their grandeur. They attempt to place the king and the prophet of Israel in a position of servitude.[4] However, as we have seen, it is Naaman who

---

1 Cohn, 'Form and Perspective', pp. 174-75, points to the irony of how quickly words from the lowliest reach the ears of the king.
2 This is clearly perceived by Ronald S. Wallace, *Elijah and Elisha: Expositions from the Book of Kings* (Edinburgh: Oliver and Boyd, 1957), p. 133. It should be noted that Naaman does not appear to be moved by any sense of obligation to take presents to the man of God, as in 1 Sam. 9.7, for he goes to the king, not the prophet. Furthermore he seems to regard the prophet's working of miracles more as a service to be bought than as a ministry to be gifted.
3 Von Rad, 'Naaman', p. 49, appreciates the import of the letter's being addressed to the king: If there is healing in Israel, then the king must be in charge of it. Also see Ellul, *Politics of God*, pp. 28-29, and Brueggemann, *2 Kings*, p. 20, who refers to the king as the 'normal health care delivery system'.
4 Cohn, 'Form and Perspective', pp. 175, 181, sees the role of Naaman's gifts as serving only the Gehazi episode.

2. The Stories in Literary-Aesthetic Perspective 75

must become a servant.

When Naaman's initiative comes up short,¹ the initiative of Elisha begins to take charge of the story. The prophet's entrance onto the stage directly follows the exclamation of the Israelite king: 'Am I God to give life and death?' (v. 7). The outcry registers not only the king's helplessness but also the underlying assumption that God does indeed wield sufficient power.² It is a rather obtrusive hint that Naaman's healing will come from a divine source. It turns our attention from human power to God's, thus preparing us for the appearance of Elisha, 'the man of God' (איש־האלהים) (v. 8).³

In v. 10 Naaman is quite prepared for Elisha's appearance. When he stations himself at the prophet's door, he is flabbergasted that only a messenger comes out to meet him. He is upset by virtually everything that happens at Elisha's threshold, yet the prophet's failure to come out to him seems to bother him most. His statement of protest is quite revealing. 'I thought⁴ to me he would surely come out!' (v. 11). The sentence achieves grammatical emphasis not only from the use of the absolute infinitive but also from the anterior positioning of אלי ('to me'). This rhetorical exposure reveals Naaman's presumption that he is Elisha's social superior and deserves the prophet's obeisance. Naaman's words, 'I thought to me he would surely come out', stand over against Elisha's words, 'let him come to me' (v. 8). As Naaman's attendants look on, he shifts attention away from his opening pout to Elisha's leprosy-healing procedure,⁵ as if *this* were responsible for his

---

1 Von Rad, 'Naaman', p. 49, observes the stalemate of Naaman's situation. Cohn, 'Form and Perspective', p. 175, sees Naaman's itinerary reaching a 'dead end', signalled by the Masoretic marking.
2 See Hobbs, *2 Kings*, p. 64, who points out that Yahweh's power to wound and to heal, to kill and to make alive is lifted up in Israel's covenant (Deut. 32.39).
3 Cohn, 'Form and Perspective', p. 176, helpfully points out the direct contrast between the king's 'Am I God?' and Elisha's epithet 'man of God'.
4 Cohn, 'Form and Perspective', draws attention to how the narrative takes us into Naaman's mind.
5 Apparently Naaman is referring to a practice of exorcism known throughout the ancient Near East. See Françoise Smith-Florentin,

rage. Yet the true cause of his anger is rather thinly veiled. The rivers of Israel and Aram provide him with a convenient opportunity to strike back without having blatantly to expose his own egocentricity. In declaring the superiority of Aram's rivers, he can subtly assert the superiority of Aram over Israel and his own superiority over an Israelite prophet.

Naaman ends his tirade in a rhetorical question in v. 12, repeating the predicates used by Elisha's messenger, 'Could I not wash in them [the Aramean rivers] and be clean?' After Naaman's turning and storming away, his servants approach him with a rhetorical question of their own. 'If the prophet had enjoined you to do some great thing', they ask, 'would you not be doing it? How much the more when he has bidden you, "Wash and be clean"?' (v. 13). The question beautifully penetrates to the heart of Naaman's hang-up. Aimed at pointing up the reasonableness of Elisha's request,[1] the question unwittingly, it seems, accomplishes much more. It exposes Naaman's obsession with greatness. The thrust of the servants' logic is that something small is easier to perform than something great. However, for Naaman the opposite is the case. This great man (איש גדול) left Aram prepared to do something great, and if Elisha had asked him to do 'a great thing' (דבר גדול), indeed, his servants are right, he would be doing it![2]

Evidently the words of his servants cause a transformation in Naaman's thinking, for the very next line finds the Aramean at Jordan's bank (v. 14). The verb ירד (go down) expresses more than physical descent. Naaman is also descending from his attitude of superiority.[3] As he lowers himself into Jordan's muddy waters he is also lowering himself in obedience to God's prophet. It is significant that Naaman's

---

'Histoire de la guérison et de la conversion de Naaman', *Foi et Vie* 69 (1970), pp. 31-33.
1 Ellul, *Politics of God*, p. 31, discusses how such reasoning is suited to this 'man of the world'. See also Fretheim, *Deuteronomistic History*, p. 153.
2 Cohn, 'Form and Perspective', p. 177, makes the connection with 'great man' in v. 1, as does Fretheim, *Deuteronomistic History*, p. 153.
3 This is noted by Hobbs, *2 Kings*, p. 69.

2. *The Stories in Literary-Aesthetic Perspective* 77

comparison to 'a little servant' (נער קטן) immediately follows the observation that he has acted 'according to the word of the man of God'.[1] The man who had been willing to do only something great (גדול) has made himself small (קטן). By bringing himself under the authority of 'the word of the man of God' he has made himself a servant (נער).

An Aramean leper finally has his flesh restored in the waters of a murky river, completing the pattern begun at the outset. Everything effectual in bringing Naaman to his healing comes from lowly sources. A captive servant girl, a prophet's servant, even his own servants serve as the instruments which lead him to deliverance.[2] The words of kings have come to nothing, while words from lowly persons have prevailed.

The scene that follows depicts the consummation of Naaman's inner transformation, the change which has taken place beneath his skin. The verb שוב occurs strategically to place this internal transformation over against the external. In v. 14 we are told that his flesh was 'restored' (שב), and then v. 15 begins by telling us that he 'returned' (שב). The narrative has once again employed a verb which suggests more than physical movement, for this verb is used often in the Old Testament to connote spiritual conversion. Even though it is used in its physical sense here, the surrounding context clearly calls forth its spiritual overtones.[3]

The Aramean's second encounter with the prophet is radically different from the first.[4] Naaman does not halt at a dis-

---

1 The significance of the phrase 'a little servant' is reinforced by the fact that it occurs as a conspicuous addition to words repeated from v. 10.
2 This is recognized by Hobbs (*2 Kings*, p. 60) and also Ellul (*Politics of God*, p. 31) who appreciates that Naaman too plays a key role in his own success through a series of decisions which could have gone differently.
3 Cohn, 'Form and Perspective', p. 178, notes the spiritual overtones. Taking this conversionary thrust as the key to the whole story are Smith-Florentin, 'Conversion de Naaman', and H. Schult, 'Naaman's Übertritt zum Yahwismus', *Dielheimer Blätter zum AT* 9 (1975), pp. 2-20.
4 Cohn, 'Form and Perspective', p. 178, points out that this section records the first real dialogue of the story.

tance and wait for Elisha to approach him as before. Instead he comes and 'stands before him' (v. 15). Naaman has at last fulfilled the words of the servant girl in v. 3; he is 'before the prophet in Israel'.[1] The phrase 'stand before' (עמד לפני), even more explicitly than the preposition by itself, conveys the notion of service or submission. And in the very next verse Elisha will use these same words to express his submission before God: 'As the Lord lives, before whom I stand' (v. 16).[2] Clearly, Naaman has entered the sphere of the prophet's authority. Thus he acknowledges himself before Elisha five times in this scene by the unequivocal term עבדך ('your servant').[3] Without a doubt, a leper has become a servant.

Naaman's identification of himself as Elisha's servant coincides with his confession of faith, 'Behold I know that there is no God in all the earth but in Israel' (v. 15). This declaration of monotheism is significant in the way it transcends Elisha's earlier statement in v. 8. Naaman now acknowledges not only the prophet, but also the God behind the prophet and behind even his own military success, as reported in v. 1.[4]

What Naaman originally brought to Israel as a lordly payment he now offers to Elisha as 'a gift (ברכה) from your servant (עבדך)' (v. 15).[5] Nevertheless, Elisha flatly refuses: 'As the Lord lives, before whom I stand, I will receive none' (v. 16). The prophet's answer underscores for Naaman that he does not stand before an exorcist who requires payment, but rather a God who requires submission. The idiom of submission (לפני) which has dominated the story is here set within a theological context.[6] The entire scene is dominated by theological emphasis. Elisha's name or generic designation, 'prophet' (נביא), does not occur here but is replaced by the more theologically

---

1 *Ibid.*
2 Hobbs, *2 Kings*, p. 66, draws attention to this repetition between vv. 15 and 16; Cohn does not.
3 Gunkel, *Elisa*, p. 39, takes note of this.
4 Fretheim, *Deuteronomistic History*, p. 151, makes a similar observation, as does Cohn, 'Form and Perspective', p. 178, and Gunkel, *Elisa*, p. 38.
5 Cohn, 'Form and Perspective', p. 178, calls this 'tribute' from a new vassal.
6 *Op. cit.*, p. 179.

2. The Stories in Literary-Aesthetic Perspective 79

explicit title, 'man of God'.¹ The prophet recedes, even as he did in the performance of the miracle, in order to direct Naaman's attention to the divine source.² Evidently he succeeds in this, for Naaman responds by asking for two loads of earth with which to build a homeland altar for worshiping Yahweh (v. 17).³ There is irony here. This man who had turned up his nose at Israel's waters is humbly (use of the particle נא) asking for Israelite soil.⁴ Moreover this leader who had strutted to Israel with a proud load of riches is leaving with a humble cargo of dirt.

A second request shows how seriously Naaman takes his new servanthood, insofar as he feels compelled to address its ramifications for his role as servant to the king of Aram. Sensing the incompatibility between his new-found faith and continuing to worship his native deity, he meekly requests pardon for escorting his lord (אדני) on future trips to the pagan temple, framing his request with the self-reference 'your servant' (עבדך) (v. 18). The repetition of his request might suggest his stumbling nervousness.⁵ Earlier Naaman had evoked an

---

1 This point is made by Fretheim, *Deuteronomistic History*, p. 146. Seeing this intention in the shift from other titles to this epithet challenges those who would take this as evidence of redaction. So, for example, Hans C. Schmitt, *Elisa: Traditionsgeschichtliche Untersuchungen zur vorklassischen nordisraelitischen Prophetie* (Gütersloh: Gerd Mohn, 1972), p. 79.
2 Ellul, *Politics of God*, pp. 32-34, draws attention to how the narrative denies credit to any one source, even Elisha. God's agency is revealed in his orchestration of a host of agents, showing his delicate relation to human freedom.
3 Wallace, *Elijah and Elisha*, p. 137, makes a helpful comment: 'Elisha had been offered a chance for a little bit of Syria in Israel and had refused it and now Naaman was taking a little bit of Israel to Syria!'
4 Cohn, 'Form and Perspective', p. 178, notes this.
5 James A. Montgomery, *A Critical and Exegetical Commentary on the Book of Kings* (International Critical Commentary; Edinburgh: T. & T. Clark, 1951), p. 375, considers the possibility of textual corruption, but Cohn, 'Form and Perspective', p. 179, strengthens the MT reading by noting its chiastic structure. At the center stands a reference to Naaman's hand, the import of which Cohn takes to be the later reference in v. 20, in which Gehazi expresses his plan to steal from that hand. Perhaps the more significant connection is with God's hand in v. 1. There Naaman did not see that God's hand

ejaculation of fear from Israel's king, but now Israel's God has put Naaman on the defensive. When Elisha responds with the blessing, 'Go in peace' (לך לשלום), it does not suggest cheap theological compromise, but rather a recognition of the realism and integrity of Naaman's commitment.[1] A theological victory has been won. Naaman has come under the authority of Yahweh. Thus the submission of Naaman is complete. Israel has prevailed on all levels: personal, national, and theological. The prophet of Israel, the land of Israel, and most of all the God of Israel all command Naaman's submission and respect.

The remaining verses of the chapter (vv. 20-27) reveal their interdependence with the preceding by a structure which is strikingly parallel to the previous episode. As before, a servant (1) journeys to a foreign person to satisfy a desire which is set forth in an opening servant-speech, (2) has that desire met through the help of servants, and (3) returns to the prophet Elisha, who renders a concluding judgment with a solemn pronouncement.[2]

Gehazi, the character who will dominate this movement as Naaman dominated the first, is promptly introduced for us in v. 20 as נער, 'servant' of Elisha, the man of God. The word נער immediately puts us in touch with that which has gone before.[3] The words of Gehazi, which quickly follow, put us in touch with that which is to come. As in the first movement, an opening speech establishes the goal toward which the narrative will move. Gehazi's monologue reveals his intention to get some of the loot that Elisha turned down. To express his aim, the servant in v. 20 repeats the oath formula used by his master, 'As the Lord lives, I will run after him and get something from him'. Yet Gehazi does not repeat Elisha's vow precisely but makes an interesting and revealing deletion. Elisha

permitted what his hand did, but now he does.
1 For particularly discerning comments in this vein, see von Rad, 'Naaman', p. 54, and Ellul, *Politics of God*, pp. 38-40.
2 For other views of the structure of the passage, see Cohn, 'Form and Perspective', pp. 171-72; Brueggemann, *2 Kings*, p. 22; Hobbs, *2 Kings*, p. 59.
3 Cohn, 'Form and Perspective', p. 180, contrasts this reference with 'the little maid' (v. 2).

2. The Stories in Literary-Aesthetic Perspective 81

in v. 16 had said, 'As the Lord lives, before whom I stand', but Gehazi does not follow the prophet in expressing submission before Yahweh.[1] What Gehazi does not say, says much. Indeed the action he is planning illustrates his lack of submission before Yahweh. By contradicting the authority of the prophet, Gehazi has ceased to 'stand before Yahweh'.

Gehazi has determined to catch up with the departing Naaman and 'get something from him' (v. 20). There is tragic irony in this oath statement, for Gehazi will get Naaman's leprosy! It is as if Gehazi has unwittingly cursed himself. Thus the ultimate fate of Gehazi is anticipated unwittingly by an opening speech, just as was the fate of Naaman in the previous sequence.

Gehazi's encounter with Naaman is significant in the way it reveals Naaman's transformed character. We find the Aramean graciously descending (נפל) from his chariot at the mere sight of the running servant (v. 21). No longer does he wait for an Israelite to approach him, but he takes the initiative, lowering himself to approach Gehazi with greeting.

Counter to Naaman, Gehazi is in the ascendant, and the narrative is careful to show this. In v. 23, when Naaman accedes to Gehazi's request,[2] he lays the gifts upon two of his own servants who then carry the merchandise before (לפני) Gehazi. Clearly Gehazi has assumed the posture of a lord.[3] The effect is heightened by the fact that, while in Naaman's presence, Gehazi feigns servanthood, referring to Elisha as 'my lord' (אדני) and to himself as having been sent as a messenger.[4] What follows may involve a reinforcing wordplay. The transfer of booty takes place when Gehazi and Naaman's servants reach העפל, translated 'the hill' (v. 24). It is

---

1 *Ibid.* Cohn sees this and contrasts 'not standing before' Yahweh with 'running after' Naaman. Hobbs (*2 Kings*, p. 67) notes the similarity but not the contrast between the oaths.
2 *Ibid.* Cohn contrasts Elisha's reaction to Naaman's 'urging' (v. 16) and Gehazi's response to his 'urging' (v. 23). Hobbs, *2 Kings*, p. 62, simply notes the parallel wording.
3 Gehazi is described as a 'lord' by von Rad, 'Naaman', p. 54, and Gunkel, *Elisa*, p. 43.
4 Cohn, 'Form and Perspective', p. 181, draws attention to the contrast between Naaman's true commissioning and Gehazi's false commissioning.

a rare form of the verb 'to swell' and in certain hiphil forms it is used to connote arrogance.[1] It does not seem unlikely that the narrative is using this particular word to draw attention to Gehazi's swelling disposition as he accepts the costly presents.[2] In much the same way, we remember, the narrative used a special verb to illustrate Naaman's descending disposition as he was experiencing his moment of truth.

In the final scene Gehazi, who has hidden his gains from sight,[3] enters and stands 'before his lord' (v. 25). Here, however, the narrative employs a different, much less common idiom to express Gehazi's posture. The preposition אל not לפני is used, so that the phrase could be rendered, 'he stood opposite his lord'.[4] Gehazi wants to pass himself off as a servant, but the narrator knows differently, and so does the prophet. Elisha quickly shows that he has not been fooled. He pronounces the curse of leprosy upon Gehazi as if it were not an arbitrary punishment but a specific consequence of the servant's action. Indeed Gehazi's own mouth had spoken it. Contrasting the prophetic blessing which had concluded Naaman's quest, a prophetic curse brings Gehazi's quest to an end.

We are told at last, 'he went out from before him a leper, like snow' (v. 27). Thus Gehazi, in departing 'from before' (מלפני) his master, accomplishes in the physical sense what he has already accomplished in the spiritual. A servant has become a leper.[5]

The entire narrative presents itself as a balanced whole. Symmetrical episodes trace the movement of two antithetical characters; a ruler moves to his deliverance, while a servant

---

1 Charles F. Burney, *Notes on the Hebrew Text of the Book of Kings* (Oxford: Clarendon, 1903), p. 282.
2 Hobbs, *2 Kings*, p. 67, sees a play on the homophone האפל, 'darkness', to draw attention to the darkness of Gehazi's deed.
3 Cohn, 'Form and Perspective', p. 181, ingeniously suggests that the absence of the direct objects of the verbs 'took' and 'deposited' in connection with the booty (v. 24) emphasizes the surreptitious nature of Gehazi's actions.
4 This insight was not my own but belongs to Cohn, 'Form and Perspective', p. 182.
5 The inclusio is recognized by Fretheim, *Deuteronomistic History*, p. 146; Jones, *1 and 2 Kings*, II, p. 412; Cohn, 'Form and Perspective', p. 183; Gressmann, *Prophetie*, p. 297.

2. The Stories in Literary-Aesthetic Perspective   83

moves to his downfall. The story pivots on the visit of a foreign general. Three Israelites react, each in a different way. The king perceives the event as a national threat, while a servant sees it as a personal opportunity. Only the prophet interprets Naaman's visit correctly. Over against the king's distress he shows resolute calmness (v. 8), and over against his servant's greed he shows disdain for the idea of trying to capitalize on such a situation (v. 26). He alone recognizes the theological import of the occasion, and in a scene which falls between Naaman's proud arrival and humble departure, he succeeds in leading the foreign dignitary to submission before Yahweh.

However, the theological meaning of the event is emphasized again at the end of the narrative, when Elisha confronts his greedy servant with the question:

> Was it a time to get money and to get garments and olive orchards and vineyards, sheep and oxen, menservants and maidservants? (v. 26).[1]

With this closing question the narrative is obviously concerned that the theological meaning of Naaman's healing not be missed. And by posing the question in this way the narrative is showing confidence that it has already given the answer. What kind of time is it? A time when Aramean generals are amassing spoils of war (to include the little Hebrew maid in v. 2), and thus a time when opportunistic Israelites are tempted to return the favor. However, a prophet in Israel has understood that this is a time when Yahweh is showing Israel a radically different way of salvation. And it is a lesson which transcends national as well as individual interests, for the

---

1 Reconciling the tension between this extended list of commodities and the fact that Gehazi got only money and garments, the Septuagint and Vulgate support the reading, 'Now you have gotten money, and you will get...?' See Montgomery, *Kings*, p. 378. Cohn, 'Form and Perspective', p. 182, suggests that the MT reading is an intentional use of 'a formulaic list of royal plunder', such as we find in 1 Sam. 8.14-17. See also Hobbs, *2 Kings*, p. 68, who calls it 'a catalog of wealth and property'. I would suggest from the context that it more specifically designates spoils of war. Accordingly, a reference to Gehazi's 'maidservants' here at the end of the story would parallel the reference to Naaman's 'little maid' at the beginning of the story.

84   *God Saves*

deliverance of an Aramean and the judgment of an Israelite pointedly reveal that God's salvation for all consists in servanthood 'before the Lord'.

2 Kings 6.8-23

2 Kgs 6.8-23 is a story full of surprises. The story begins abruptly. Instead of an initiating verb, as is usual in Hebrew narration, we first meet the subject, who will generate the ensuing action. The king of Aram, we are told, is making war against Israel. More specific identification of this king and this conflict are not given.[1] We are not led from this statement to the battlefield but to the council chamber where the king's war plans are being discussed with his servants. No specifics are disclosed here, only generic information about the king's decision to locate his camp 'at such and such a place (מקום)', apparently for ambush (v. 8).

The next verse records a second exchange of military information, this time from the side of Israel (v. 9). The initiator of this exchange is not the opposing king but rather 'the man of God' (איש האלהים), who informs the king of Israel as to the enemy's location. The word 'place' (מקום) designates the enemy's location here as it did in the previous verse, suggesting the accuracy of the information, even while maintaining the generic quality of the narration. How this informant comes by his information we are not yet told, but his identification as a man 'of God' is suggestive.

The first word of this man of God, 'Be on guard!' (השמר), does not at first seem particularly noteworthy. However, when the sound of this word is repeated in the ensuing statement (שם ארם) it is at least enough to cause *us* to 'be on guard' for any special emphasis which may be in the making.[2]

---

1 For an attempt to date the conflict on indirect evidence, see Gray, *Kings*, pp. 512-13. By contrast, Hobbs, *2 Kings*, p. 76, sees the reference to Aramean warfare as serving a thematic rather than a chronological purpose. He remarks, 'The lack of interest in dating is shown by the absence of the names of the kings involved'. See also Brueggemann, *2 Kings*, p. 24.

2 This 'rhyme' is acknowledged by LaBarbera, 'Man of War', p. 640, who goes on to see additional emphasis on this verb in the narrative,

2. *The Stories in Literary-Aesthetic Perspective* 85

Keenly alerted, the king of Israel is now ready for royal initiative. He sends 'to the place (מקום) of which the man of God has spoken' and warns it (v. 10). This is conveyed with the same brevity and generality which has marked the narration up to this point. Any thought of using such military intelligence for offensive purposes is not even raised; Israel is clearly the threatened party and completely on the defensive.

The following phrase plainly rounds off this opening section. We are simply told that the king of Israel 'was on guard there (נשמר שם) more than once or twice' (v. 10). The adverbial phrase here explicitly generalizes the preceding scenario in line with the generalizing tendency already noted. The verb here is especially notworthy. It repeats the verb by which the Israelite king was warned in v. 9[1] and, as happened in that verse, it is here closely followed by a homophonic expression (שם).[2] Thus the repetition of the entire section combines to highlight this verb. The verb's own meaning may suggest an additional dimension of significance. While the niphal form here can be translated 'he was on guard', in line with its sense in v. 9, it can also be rendered 'he was preserved'.[3] This rendering is probably better in suiting the apparent resolving effect of the statement.

The thrust of this entire introductory section can now be put into focus. First we hear that the Aramean king is making war, and finally we hear that Israel's king is being preserved. In between, strategic information about the place (מקום) of planned attack is conveyed three times. Standing at the center and flanked on either side by royal communications, is the word of the man of God. This figure who stands between the two kings in this literary context also stands between them in the actual military context, keeping any attack from transpiring. While his source of information has not yet been explicitly disclosed, for the time being, his word represents the balance of power.

Following this typical scenario, the rest of the narrative

as we shall see below.
1 Jones, *Kings*, p. 425, draws attention to this.
2 LaBarbera, 'Man of War', p. 640, points to this.
3 So AV and RSV, in contrast to NEB, NASB, and NIV, which retain the sense of 'guarded'.

(vv. 11-23) presents a particular episode which can be seen as an expanded variation on the same sequence.[1] Again we begin with a threatening military initiative by the Aramean king and end with a disarming counter-measure by the Israelite king. And as before, the man of God stands between them, both literarily and militarily, and holds the key to a bloodless resolution. While the framework is familiar, the content is full of surprises, as brevity and generality give way to expansion and particularity.

Whereas the introductory section (vv. 8-10) took us first into the Aramean king's secret military council, the beginning of this section penetrates even further into Aramean intelligence, exposing the king's very mind (לב) (v. 11). We learn that he is troubled about 'this matter', that is, the pattern of Aramean failure which has just been described. In turning 'to his servants' (אל־עבדיו), as he had before, another military initiative is signalled, but now internal suspicions take precedence over external strategies. The king asks, 'Will you not tell me which of us[2] is for the king of Israel?' (v. 11). The reluctance of the king to bring blunt accusation before his trusted men is reflected in the way second-person reference is first softened by the use of the indicative instead of the imperative and then avoided entirely by the king's inclusion of himself among the suspects.

The response from one of the servants is at first reassuring and respectful, 'None, my lord, O king' (v. 12). However, reassurance quickly gives way to a disturbing revelation, for this spokesman somehow knows where the Israelite king is getting his information. The informant is identified not generically, as before, but specifically and personally as 'Elisha, the prophet who is in Israel'. Witholding the name of Elisha until this point in the narrative produces an interesting effect, in view of the meaning of Elisha's name, *namely*, 'God delivers'. Who is for the king of Israel? 'None', says the Aramean servant, 'but "God delivers"'. The full context of the servant's

1 Similarly Brueggemann, *2 Kings*, p. 24; in contrast to LaBarbera, 'Man of War', p. 639; Hobbs, *2 Kings*, pp. 73-74.
2 Some versions, instead of 'which of us', read 'who has betrayed us' (see BHS note). For a clear discussion of the evidence, which finds no compelling reason not to retain the MT, see Jones, *Kings*, p. 425.

2. The Stories in Literary-Aesthetic Perspective   87

remark certainly obscures this unwitting effect, but this is fitting in that there is more truth here than Aramean intelligence has yet uncovered. On the other hand, the servant's claim that Elisha passes along what the Aramean king 'speaks in his bedroom' certainly points beyond any ordinary intelligence capability. This reference is also significant in contributing to the feeling of infiltration which dominates this scene.[1] Not just the royal council chamber but even the royal bedroom, yes, the king's very mind has been infiltrated.

Armed with new information, the Aramean monarch can again strike out with kingly imperatives. 'Go and see where he is', the servants are told (v. 13). Interestingly, there appears no hint of doubt that this man who knows the location of the Arameans can be located. Even more interesting is the confidence which the king shows in the result clauses which follow his imperatives. The Aramean servants are to find Elisha, 'so that I may send (שלח) and seize (לקח) him' (v. 13). Earlier Elisha and the king of Israel had been the subject of the verb שלח (vv. 9, 10); now the Aramean king lays claim to such administrative action. The entire imperative/result-clause sequence projects the assumption that the seizure of Elisha depends entirely upon knowledge of his whereabouts. In one sense, the king's session with his advisors ends as it began, with the king placing responsibility at the door of his intelligence operation.

As if to suggest the efficiency of Aramean intelligence, the report on Elisha's location comes back with lightning quickness and crispness, with no words wasted: 'And it was told him, "Behold, in Dothan"' (v. 13). Now the earlier confidence of the king of Aram will have the chance to prove itself. The beginning of the next statement lives up to the royal claims; we are told, 'He sent (שלח) to that place (שם)' (v. 14). The use of שלח signals the follow-through of the royal plan (v. 13). The term שם, used twice in the opening section to indicate and emphasize the place which has 'been guarded' (נשמר) from attack, is now placed squarely within Aramean sights. However, the rest of v. 14 may raise a degree of suspicion

---

1 As Hobbs, *2 Kings*, p. 77, points out, this reference functions as an idiomatic expression for secrecy, as in Eccl. 10.20.

about the king's confidence. In order to capture one man, the king dispatches 'horses, chariots and a great army'. On the other hand, we would have to know more about the potential for military resistance before we could be sure that this represented nervous over-kill. One might speculate that a military resource as valuable as Elisha would have generated precautionary protection. At any rate, the Aramean military initiative, which we have viewed from its inception, is here brought to the threshold of its moment of truth, as Aramean soldiers surround a sleeping city.

As happened in the introductory section (v. 9), the scene now shifts abruptly from the Aramean side to the Israelite. Just as the foregoing scene was generated by the Aramean king's interaction with his servants, here the scene develops from interaction between Elisha and his servant. In contrast to the Arameans' calculated nocturnal approach, Elisha's unsuspecting servant 'arose early and went out' (v. 15). He is identified as the servant of 'the man of God'; the narrative picks up the term used to designate Elisha when his success over the Arameans was being described in the opening section (vv. 9, 10). There the Arameans had been unable to surprise Israel, but now Elisha's own servant is shocked with the sight of Arameans in all directions: 'Behold, an army with horses and chariots was surrounding the city' (v. 15). The Arameans, it seems, had finally gotten the jump on Israel. The Aramean servants' intelligence report, 'Behold, in Dothan' (v. 13), now can be seen over against an Israelite servant's alarm, 'Behold, an army'. Now it is time for the Israelite side to ask, 'What (איכה) shall we do?' The interrogative adverb used here by Elisha's servant echoes the one used earlier (v. 13) by Aram's king in reference to Elisha: 'Where (איכה) is he?'[1] Whereas the earlier query had constituted Aramean action, the present query represents Israelite *reaction*.

The mood changes abruptly with Elisha's answer. Whereas the Aramean king needed reassurance *from* his servants, Elisha offers reassurance *to* his servant. 'Fear not',[2] he says,

---

1 Reinforcing this connection is the rarity of the specific pointing of this first reference. See *Hebrew and English Lexicon*, p. 32.
2 Hobbs, *2 Kings*, p. 77, sees this imperative in relation to the formu-

2. The Stories in Literary-Aesthetic Perspective 89

'for there are more with us than with them' (v. 16). Elisha conveys this to his servant's ears but then asks God to reveal it to his eyes (v. 17). Elisha, who had been concerned earlier that his king 'watch' (שמר) for the enemy, is now concerned that his servant 'sees' (ראה) that which transcends the enemy. The answer to Elisha's prayer reinforces his answer to his servant's question, 'What shall we do?' This is highlighted by wordplay. It is not for this servant 'to fear' (ירא) but 'to see' (ראה).[1]

What the servant sees is startling and spectacular and completely counters what he had seen earlier: 'Behold, the mountain was filled with horses and chariots of fire surrounding Elisha' (v. 17). Aramean chariots (רכב) and horses (סוס) were surrounding (סבב) the city (v. 15), but flaming chariots (רכב) and horses (סוסים) were surrounding (סבב) Elisha. These verbal parallels between the servant's first and second revelations punctuate the military reversal. Aram's upper hand is shown to be an illusion. Noticeably lacking among the parallels of the servant's heavenly vision, however, is any mention of an army. Can it be that Elisha himself is filling this role?[2] The Aramean king's decision to send 'a great army' after one man can now be seen in a new light.

The interchange between Elisha and his servant, like the interchange between the Aramean king and his servants, gives way to military initiative. In v. 18 the military clash, which heretofore had been averted, finally takes place. Actually the narrative is ambiguous as to who makes the first move, thereby stretching out the suspense. We are simply told, *'they* came down to (אל) Elisha'. This could refer either to the Arameans' coming to attack[3] or the heavenly forces' coming to help.[4] Either way the narrative would still be showing a

---

laic expression belonging to the tradition of 'holy war' (see Gerhard von Rad, *Der heilige Krieg im Alten Israel* [Göttingen: Vandenhoeck & Ruprecht, 1952], pp. 9-10).
1 This wordplay was first noted by LaBarbera, 'Man of War', p. 642.
2 This is the suggestion of LaBarbera, 'Man of War', p. 641.
3 So RSV, which supplies 'the Syrians'.
4 LaBarbera, 'Man of War', p. 642, defends this option, arguing that the Arameans would have to 'go up' to reach Elisha on Tell Dothan. However, the descent might have to do with the relative position of

defensive posture for the forces of Israel. The statement which follows, however, teases us with the alternative. Elisha asks Yahweh to 'strike this people with blindness'. Before the prepositional phrase here, which comes last, Elisha uses a verb (נכה) which is often used to denote 'killing'.[1] In the present military context the appended qualification of the call 'to strike' the Arameans comes as an unexpected twist. A little later on, the narrative will, with this very same verb, plainly raise the issue of killing the Arameans (v. 21), so it is probably doing the same here in a more subtle way.

Without sight the Aramean army is completely dependent upon sound, and so the Arameans easily come under the sway of the one whose words have dominated the course of events from the beginning. Elisha's words first indicate negation of their secret mission. 'This is not the way and this is not the city', he tells the Arameans (v. 19). This refutation of Aramean intelligence is followed by an over-ruling of Aramean administration. Employing the imperative with which the Aramean king had initiated the mission of these soldiers (לכו), Elisha now gives them new orders. 'Go after me', he commands.[2] Highlighting this imperative are two additional occurrences of the verb הלך in the remainder of v. 19.[3] Here Elisha seizes the position of the one who had sent to seize him. The army which had 'come' (בא), under orders from the king (vv. 13-14), now 'goes' (הלך), under orders from the prophet.

Promising to take the Arameans 'to the man whom you seek' (v. 19), Elisha leads them to Samaria (שמרון). The Arameans had been told in Dothan that 'this is not the city', so special attention is now drawn to Samaria. The reference to Samaria becomes even more noteworthy in the light of its

---

mounted forces at the point of encounter. Moreover, LaBarbera's assumption that Yahweh's forces would be 'above' Elisha is not to be taken for granted, since the narrative says only that they 'surrounded' Elisha.

1 See *Hebrew and English Lexicon*, pp. 645-46.
2 LaBarbera, 'Man of War', p. 643, notes this connection and argues that the Aramean king's command is not fulfilled until this point. However, the king's command to 'go and see where Elisha is' finds fulfillment in v. 14 with the report, 'Behold in Dothan'.
3 So LaBarbera, 'Man of War', p. 643.

2. The Stories in Literary-Aesthetic Perspective 91

clear relationship to the root שמר, which was highlighted in the introductory section (vv. 9, 10).[1] There we saw how שמר had played a key role in the discussion of how Israel 'was preserved'. The connection with this section is strengthened when Samaria is mentioned twice more, in a way approaching redundancy, in the following verse (v. 20). If Samaria here reminds us of Israel's past experiences of being preserved, we are still left in wonderment about what shape the present experience will take.

Upon entering Samaria, Elisha promptly and quite unexpectedly prays the same prayer for the Aramean soldiers that he had prayed for his terrified servant: 'Yahweh, open their eyes, that they may see' (v. 20; cf. v. 17). Given their divinely induced state of blindness, this prayer now implies only a restoration of natural sight. The Arameans had earlier been commanded by their king to 'see' where Elisha was (v. 13), but now they are shown that Yahweh is the real source of authority behind their 'seeing'. Just as Elisha had shown his power over the Arameans with the use of the first imperative used by the Aramean king ('go', לכו), Yahweh now shows his power over the Arameans in relation to the second imperative used by the Aramean king ('see', ראו).[2]

When the Arameans' sight returns, the exclamation, 'Behold, in the midst of Samaria!' (v. 20), announces their revelation with a curtness which recalls their earlier revelation, 'Behold, in Dothan' (v. 13). This only accentuates the stunning reversal of their situation: the ambushers have become the ambushed. This section had begun with these Arameans 'surrounding' (סובב) one Israelite city (v. 15) and ends with them 'in the midst' (בתוך) of another.

Elisha's mastery over Aram's military position, now, as in the introductory scenario, defers to the king of Israel (v. 21). This time the king does not merely hear about Aramean soldiers but is able to 'see' (ראה) them for himself. Like the first Israelite to see this army, the king immediately and respect-

---

1 Op. cit., p. 644.
2 This connection is observed by LaBarbera, 'Man of War', p. 643, but here again he claims that the Aramean king's imperative 'see' was not fulfilled until now, despite the testimony of the latter part of v. 14.

fully[1] asks Elisha what to do, but not without registering his own preferred option: 'Shall I smite? Shall I smite, my father?' (v. 21). The verb נכה, seen earlier in Elisha's prayer (v. 18), is here used in its unqualified sense. While the repetition in the MT is awkward and there is some support for seeing either dittography or a mispointed infinitive absolute,[2] the redundancy may function to reflect the king's excited state.[3] The repetition may also function to signal a special emphasis upon this verb in the total narrative, especially in light of its earlier occurrences in v. 18 and earlier passages, perhaps, in the homophonic expressions of Elisha's servant (איכה, v. 15) and the Aramean king (אקחהו and איכה, v. 13).

The Israelite king's proposal to smite the captive Arameans may be reinforced by the literary context, but it is not reinforced by the Israelite prophet. Elisha flatly rejects his king's suggestion and follows up with a rhetorical question: 'Do you smite those whom you have taken captive with your sword and with your bow?' (v. 22). The intended effect of Elisha's question is obvious, even though its precise meaning and reasoning are not. Elisha must be arguing one of two points: (1) 'Since *your* weapons have not gotten these captives, it is improper for *you* to kill them'.[4] (2) 'If it is proper to spare ordinary captives, how much more these whom Yahweh has delivered alive'.[5] Either way, killing these captives is unequivocally not the right course of action, but Elisha, as all along, knows what is and hastens to commend it. His plan is the very

---

1 Note the expression, 'my father', which is also used by King Joash to refer to Elisha in 2 Kgs 13.14 and by Elisha to refer to Elijah in 2 Kgs 2.12. For discussions of its significance see James G. Williams, 'The Prophetic "Father"', *JBL* 85 (1966), pp. 344-48, and Anthony Phillips, 'The Ecstatics' Father', in *Words and Meanings* (ed. Peter R. Ackroyd and B. Lindars; Cambridge: Cambridge University Press, 1968), pp. 183-94.
2 See BHS note, and Burney, *Notes*, p. 287.
3 This is also suggested by Hobbs, *2 Kings*, p. 72.
4 So, e.g., Burney, *Notes*, p. 287, and Gray, *Kings*, p. 515, who find reinforcement on textual grounds. However, these textual grounds are disputed by Montgomery, *Kings*, p. 382. Cf. NEB.
5 So, e.g., William E. Barnes, *The Second Book of the Kings* (Cambridge Bible; Cambridge: Cambridge University Press, 1928), p. 29; Montgomery, *Kings*, p. 382; Hobbs, *2 Kings*, p. 78.

2. *The Stories in Literary-Aesthetic Perspective* 93

antithesis of the king's. He calls not for killing the Arameans but for feeding them (v. 22). He even specifies his intention that they return to 'their lord' (אדניהם). The authority which Elisha has demonstrated in this ordeal has not been intended to cancel completely the Aramean structures, but neither has it been intended to leave these structures unaffected.

Elisha's intentions are satisfied on all counts. The king of Israel treats the Arameans to a 'great feast' and then 'sends' (שלח) them to 'their lord' (v. 23). The use of שלח here is interesting in the way it registers a subtle concluding note of tension between Aramean and Israelite lordship. We noted earlier how that the first two verbs, which the Aramean monarch had used to dictate his military operation (v. 13), were taken up to express Israel's assumption of control over the Arameans. The use of שלח here constitutes the third verb in that series to be so used. The fourth predicate in that series, the verb 'to seize' (לקח), represents the one action in Aram's mission to remain unfulfilled by Aram and unclaimed by Israel. No one is finally captured, but everyone is finally captivated by a new vision of Yahweh's action in Israel.

The change in human perception yields a change in human history. Human action is transformed in the light of divine action. At the beginning (v. 10) we were told that Israelite evasions of Aramean ambushes had occurred 'repeatedly' (לא אחת ולא שתים), but at the end (v. 23) we are told that Aramean incursions into Israelite territory 'occurred not again' (לא־יספו עוד). In the middle the cycle is broken, because Yahweh reveals his power in spectacular and surprising ways. He shows that his power, which cannot be confined to a temporal cycle, keeps (שמר) Israelites from being confined to a spatial circle. However, this same power also preserves the Arameans when they become encircled in Samaria (שמרון). In so doing, the amazing power which Yahweh channels through his prophet keeps in balance the ordinary power of kings, in ways that all can see. Thus, Yahweh opens history by opening blinded eyes and giving fresh insight (ראה) into his enduring oversight (שמר).

In summary, the story told here has its own insight to give: Yahweh keeps (שמר) Israel. This may sound obvious, but this narrative knows that this truth is often not so obvious. A short introduction develops a recurring scenario of Yahweh's preservation of Israel from Aramean ambush without directly mentioning Yahweh's agency. Here God repeatedly preserves Israel through human agency with a subtlety which leaves his part easily overlooked. Indeed, when the narrative moves on to develop a particular episode in Aram's continuing campaign against Israel, the prophet Elisha becomes the prime target in the Arameans' sights, and Yahweh hardly shows up in Aram's trusted strategy or Israel's anxious reactions. However, in a dramatic departure from the earlier strategy by which Israel had been preserved, Yahweh breaks out of the background to manifest his saving action in spectacular and stupefying ways. The prophet, who had earlier mediated a subtle saving word in a way that drew little attention to his source, now mediates a dramatic saving vision by way of open prayer to Yahweh. A new vision (ראה) of Yahweh's power replaces the blindness of Israelites and Arameans alike. Where, as beforehand, blind servants could see only that power which seemed to give them no options, and blind monarchs could see only that power which seemed to give them all the options, there could now be acknowledged the presence of another power at work in their midst which generated new possibilities for everyone. This power, which could now be acknowledged even where it remained in the background, is not brought forward to obliterate human power. Human history and human kingdoms are seen to continue, but not without being revised and revisioned in the light of Yahweh's irresistible power to preserve whom he will.[1]

---

1 After I had completed this section, another treatment of 2 Kgs 6.8-23 appeared from Walter Brueggemann, 'The Embarrassing Footnote', *Theology Today* 44 (1987), pp. 5-14. Extending the brief literary-sensitive analysis which he gives this passage in his commentary, Brueggemann further elaborates his understanding of the social function of the story along the lines of LaBarbera's study, which he cites with approval. In addition to relating his treatment of the story to larger hermeneutical issues, Brueggemann goes beyond LaBarbera in at least two ways. First, like my own study, Brueggemann's analysis better appreciates how the story moves beyond negative social criticism to illuminate positive theological claims which propose to open history. Secondly, Brueggemann thinks LaBarbera is not 'radical enough' in his perception of this social criticism. The

2. The Stories in Literary-Aesthetic Perspective 95

2 Kings 6.24–7.20

2 Kgs 6.24–7.20 tells a gripping story. An Aramean army places a stranglehold upon an Israelite city.[1] Within the besieged city a desperate Israelite king closes in upon a prophet of God. Outside the city a desperate quartet of lepers, who feel death closing in on every side, get a grip on themselves to become instrumental in a divinely orchestrated salvation.

The story is told in two movements: the first introduces and elaborates the problem; the second introduces and traces out the solution. These contrasting themes are established at the beginning of each movement by a parallel literary structure. In 6.25 the Aramean siege has brought about the situation that

> an ass's head was sold for eighty shekels of silver,
> a quarter of a kab of dove's dung for five shekels of silver.

In 7.1 the prophet Elisha prophesies for the next day the situation that

> a measure of flour will sell for a shekel,
> and two measures of barley for a shekel in the gate of Samaria.

Both poetic parallelisms stand forth from their prose surroundings to command deserved attention. Thus, the first

---

narrative aims not just 'to expose or make fun of the royal arrangement', says Brueggemann, but to render it 'completely nullified' (p. 16 n. 9). In pressing his point this way, Brueggemann obscures the more nuanced portrayal of royal authority structures which I have shown. Aramean and Israelite structures are not so completely lumped together nor so 'completely nullified' as Brueggemann here indicates. Could it be that Brueggemann's sociological emphasis courts a reductionistic tendency which is here suppressing the more flexible thrust of the theological dimension of the story, which Brueggemann himself otherwise appreciates so well?

1 Hobbs, *2 Kings*, p. 79, who connects this story with the preceding one, argues that the Aramean king now launches a full scale war against Samaria ('he mustered all his forces', v. 24) in contrast to the border raids which had been discontinued (v. 23). By contrast, most scholars would take these references as evidence that these stories are *not* meant to be seen in chronological sequence.

movement is overshadowed by the sword of the Arameans; the second movement is overshadowed by the word of the Lord.

In both movements an episode of desperate action follows an introductory saying. In the first movement we follow the actions of the king within the city (6.26-33),[1] in the second we follow the actions of four lepers outside the city (7.3-20). The two poles of the social order stand over against each other.

For both parties, a question introduces and stands behind their actions. The king asks, 'If Yahweh will not help you,[2] how can I help you?' (6.27). The lepers ask, 'Why do we sit here until we die?' (7.3). Whereas the former question expresses human helplessness[3] and holds divine inaction responsible, the latter points the way toward human responsiveness by sharing responsibility for personal inaction.

Both parties later make contrasting declarations which constitute the respective turning points of the two movements. The king swears to behead Elisha that very 'day' (יום, 6.31). The lepers, on the other hand, decide that taking their good news to the king was the order of the 'day' (יום, 7.9).

Contrast between the king and the lepers is manifest throughout the respective episodes. The king's actions are solitary and destructive. When met with a simple petition for

1 While the king is identified as 'Benhadad', this name was borne by several kings of Damascus. See Hobbs, *2 Kings*, pp. 78-79. It seems to be the case that the narrative is here using Benhadad as a generic name, proper to Aramean kings of the period; cf. Benjamin Mazar, 'The Aramean Empire and its Relations with Israel', *BA* (1962), p. 106; and William F. Albright, 'A Votive Stele Erected by Benhadad I of Damascus to the God of Melcarth', *BASOR* 89 (1942), p. 28.
2 The context would lead one to expect here a conditional clause. This has frequently led to the proposal to emend אל to אם לא. Montgomery, *Kings*, pp. 388-89, prefers to accept the MT as an exclamatory negative: 'No! May the eternal help you!' Gray, *Kings*, p. 519, has offered a more credible solution. He gives precedents for the use of the jussive to form the protasis of a conditional sentence and reads אל here as the natural negative before a jussive verb.
3 Ellul, *Politics of God*, p. 44, recognizes that ישע can be rendered 'to save' as well as 'to help' and thinks that the woman's cry and the king's response are both meant to register an ambiguity between physical help and salvation before God.

2. The Stories in Literary-Aesthetic Perspective 97

help, the king snaps back with angry sarcasm—'How can I help you, from the threshing floor or from the winepress?' (6.27).[1] After hearing about an act of cannibalism the king can only rend his garment and swear to sever the head of God's prophet (6.31).[2] So soon after the mention of an ass's head (6.25), there may be some irony here. The end of this episode returns us to the beginning with the king blaming and questioning God for his inaction: 'This trouble is from Yahweh! Why should I wait for Yahweh any longer (עוד)?' (6.33).[3]

The lepers cannot wait for themselves any longer, until they die (עד־מחנו, 7.3)! Their actions, by contrast, are co-operative and constructive. After reasonably considering their options, they pursue the only ray of hope left to them, going over to the Aramean camp (7.4).[4] The fact that the Arameans mistake the approaching lepers for kings (7.6) lends literary support to comparing these lepers with the king of Israel. Another literary subtlety serves to enhance the irony of the Arameans' distorted detection of intruders, for they mistake the lepers, מצרעים, for kings of Egypt, מצרים (7.6).[5]

Obviously, the lepers' co-operation and benevolence[6] are in

---

1 Perhaps the reference to the king's location on 'the wall' (חמה), a reference conspicuously repeated in v. 30, would draw attention to the king's anger (חמה). There also may be some significance to the mention of the threshing floor. Hobbs, *2 Kings*, p. 80, points out that 'the threshing floor in Samaria was at the gate (1 Kings 22.10)'. The relevance of this fact will be shown later.
2 Ellul, *Politics of God*, p. 47, helpfully points to the contradiction of invoking the authority of God in order to reject that authority in the form of the prophet.
3 Brueggemann, *2 Kings*, p. 27, acknowledges an ironic contrast between these two references to Yahweh. Here in v. 33 the king refuses to depend any longer on Yahweh, but in v. 27 he conceded that no one but Yahweh could help.
4 LaBarbera, 'Man of War', p. 648, makes the interesting point that the action of these lepers, whose condition disqualifies them from military service (see Lev. 13 and 14), is expressed with a verb (נפל) which is used often in military contexts to connote either the act of desertion or attack. He sees an intentional irony here.
5 LaBarbera, 'Man of War', p. 649, takes note of this pun.
6 Hobbs, *2 Kings*, p. 91, is right to point out that the lepers are not without the motivation of 'fear of reprisals'. See Ellul, *Politics of God*, pp. 64-65.

contrast with the social upheaval in the city.¹ While those within the city are making decisions to devour each other, both figuratively (6.31)² and literally (6.29), the four lepers outside the city act to save themselves and then the city with decisions which arise in each case out of mutually supportive dialogue: 'each said to his companion' (7.3, repeated in v. 9). This contrast is reinforced by wordplay. The king is prompted to destructive reaction by 'the evil' (הרעה) (6.33), but each of the lepers is prompted to saving action by 'his companion' (רעהו). Another specific contrast is seen between the woman's decision to hide her son after helping to eat her neighbor's (6.29) and the lepers' decision not to go on hiding their life-saving plunder from the starving city (7.9).

It also may be noteworthy that the Aramean soldiers are similarly shown to have acted in a mutually supportive way. When they are surprised in the night, self-destructive panic³ is avoided as 'each spoke to his brother (אחיו)'. The parallel here with the lepers seems significant, especially when the narrative finally associates the actions of the Arameans with life. At the end of 7.7 we are told that the Arameans fled for 'their life' (נפשם).⁴

Together the two movements of the story achieve a symmetry in the changing scope of dramatic action. The story begins on a wide stage, then steadily narrows to a tight focus at its midpoint, after which it progressively widens once again. Specifically, we begin with the wide scene of the Aramean army gathering around an Israelite city (6.24). A conversa-

---

1 The prophet who is locked inside his house and the elders who are 'with him' (אתו) represent one pocket of supportive community within the city (v. 32).
2 Also, as Ellul, *Politics of God*, p. 52, points out, the extraordinary prices for the most pitiful scraps is an indirect commentary on the exploitation taking place. See Wallace, *Elijah and Elisha*, p. 149.
3 Such is the effect of Gideon's surprising ruse on the Midianites (Judg. 7.22).
4 Hobbs, *2 Kings*, p. 91, wonders why the Arameans would have left their mules and horses, since they would have facilitated a quick get-away. Gray, *Kings*, p. 525, suggests fear of inadequate time to harness them. Be that as it may, it is interesting that whereas the Israelite king is reluctant to risk any of his horses in a life-saving venture, the Arameans do not hesitate.

2. The Stories in Literary-Aesthetic Perspective 99

tion from the city wall narrows the focus considerably (6.26). Then we zero in upon the most constricted scene of the story where a prophet is trapped behind the door of his house (6.32). The scope expands a notch with the outset of the second movement. We find four lepers clustered like barnacles on the side of a starving city (7.3). Their movement expands the field of vision until finally the picture of an entire city stampeding toward relief returns us to the wide scene (7.16). We can imagine a camera lens zooming in, then out again, adjusting to the changing scope of the action. It is exquisite how this dramatic effect of contraction followed by expansion draws out the theme of each movement. The constriction of the scope of action enhances the sense of the constriction of the siege, until finally our vision is focused upon an entrapped prophet, a siege within a siege. As this tight focus is released to take in wider and wider scenes, we feel ourselves moving toward the salvation of a captive city.[1] This dramatic effect is reinforced by two contrasting images which dominate the respective movements. Central to the first movement is the image of 'the wall' (החמה, 6.26, 30) and its analogue, the closed 'door' (דלח, twice in 6.32). Central to the second movement is the image of 'the opening of the gate' (פתח השער)[2] and its analogue, 'the edge of the camp' (קצה המחנה) (7.3, 8).[3] Every scene takes place against the background of these images, which themselves graphically symbolize first the closure and then the opening up of the respective episodes.

Just as we see dramatic action in terms of a horizontal dimension, we also see dramatic tension in terms of a vertical dimension. Tension consists in the subtle interplay between human and divine action. This tension is introduced with skillful literary signals in the king's opening conversation with a distressed woman (6.26). A woman cries, 'Help!' Before finding out her trouble, the king takes this as an occasion to

---

1 It is interesting to note that the root meaning of ישע is 'be wide'. See Gray, *Kings*, p. 503.
2 LaBarbera, 'Man of War', p. 645, recognizes that this second movement is 'cleverly unified by the motif of the gate'.
3 The prior analogue of 'windows in heaven' appears momentarily in the captain's skeptical response (7.2), but this serves as a foil for the image that will be pursued.

insinuate his anger over lack of help (picking up on her word
יָשַׁע) from the Lord (6.27). As his tension with God begins to
manifest itself, the king asks a little question of the woman
that the narrative uses to convey a big point about the king
(6.28). Says the king, 'What is your problem?' The Hebrew
syntax yields an interesting juxtaposition: הַמֶּלֶךְ מַה־לָּךְ. The king
wants to know the problem, and the narrative intimates that
the king *himself* is the problem! And indeed the king *is* the
problem in both movements of the story. In the first
movement he contradicts the good report implied of God's
prophet (6.33); in the second he contradicts the good report of
the lepers (7.12), thereby resisting the progress of the divine
will.[1]

Even as royal words unwittingly point out the problem, they
also unwittingly point out the solution. We see this in the
king's last statement from the top of the wall (6.31). Since the
story has not yet introduced Elisha, it comes as a surprise that
the king suddenly, without giving reason, names Elisha in an
edict of execution. I suggest that this involves a deliberate literary maneuver to exploit the meaning of Elisha's name—
אֱלִישָׁע, 'God helps'. While our ears are still ringing with a dis-
traught woman's cry of 'Help!', the narrator secures the
divine pole of dramatic tension by making a play on the name
of the prophet—'God helps'.[2]

The vertical dynamics of the human-divine tension show
the theological depth as well as the human relevance of the
story. The king's attack upon God above is turned downward.
His Highness 'descends' (ירד) upon God's servant (6.33). God's
counter movement, however, comes from below. He accomplishes his high aims through low means—through an
entrapped prophet, through outcast lepers, and through a
nameless servant who corrects the king's inadequate logic

---

1 Hobbs, *2 Kings*, p. 93, generalizes this point with respect to not only
this story but other stories in 2 Kings: 'the role of officialdom is to
frustrate the movement of the stories from problem to solution'.
2 Not only the name Elisha but also the identification 'son of Shaphat
(שָׁפָט)' may be significant to the thrust of the narrative, for God's
action to save will in the end merge with his action to judge (שָׁפַט) the
king's captain (7.17).

2. *The Stories in Literary-Aesthetic Perspective* 101

(7.13).¹ That this vertical dynamic forms the central thrust of the story becomes clear when we examine the dramatic highpoint of the narrative—the point of transition from the first movement to the last. When the prophet delivers the divine prediction of relief (7.1), there can be no doubt about the divine aim. Yet the prediction that fulfillment will occur within a day generates the question of divine means. The question 'How?' is posed in sharpest terms by the king's captain: 'If Yahweh made windows in heaven, could this thing be?' (7.2). Though laced with skepticism, for which the officer will meet judgment, the suggestion points above. God's actual means of accomplishing his word, however, will come from below, and the narrative has a way of highlighting this contrast without giving the story away. From the lofty suggestion of 'windows in heaven', ארבות בשמים (7.2), the narrative immediately shifts attention to a leprous 'quartet of men', ארבעה אנשים (7.3). The anterior positioning of the latter phrase (we would expect the new paragraph to begin with a form of היה) indicates that its verbal correspondence to 'windows in heaven' is no accident.² We are led to suspect immediately that God will use the four lepers to accomplish his transcendent intention.

Maintaining curiosity and suspense, the narrative plants other clues which connect the lepers to the prophecy of deliverance. Such a hint is given in the comment that these lepers were at the entrance of 'the gate' (שער), a place which we acknowledged earlier as the dominating image of the second movement. Elisha's prediction of deliverance in 7.1 had ended with a very conspicuous reference to 'the gate':

a measure of flour (סאה־סלח) for a shekel (בשקל)
and two measures of barley (וסאתים שערים) for a shekel (בשקל)
in the gate (בשער) of Samaria (שמרון).

The reference to the 'gate' (שער) here is made conspicuous not only because it appears as an addition in a literary structure which is repeated from 6.25,³ but also because of the allitera-

---

1 Hobbs, *2 Kings*, pp. 91-92, notices the significance here of help arising from 'lesser figures'. See also Ellul, *Politics of God*, p. 62.
2 LaBarbera, 'Man of War', p. 648, draws attention to the wordplay between 'four' and 'windows'.
3 The fact that the repetition here inclines toward a shortening rather

tion and assonance which surround it. Associating deliverance with שער triggers our anticipation when we see lepers sitting at the שער.

The gate (שער) continues to be used as a reminder of the prophecy, marking the trail, as it were, toward deliverance. When the lepers decide to publicize their life-saving discovery, they come and call to the city gate-watch, שער (7.10),[1] which in turn (7.11) informs the king's household. When the king balks at the news, his servant's suggestion to send scouts upon five of the remaining (שאר) horses, with the conspicuous reiteration of the fact that the horses remain (שאר) there, gives added reassurance to our expectations by using a homophone of שער (7.13).

When deliverance comes to pass 'according to the word of the Lord', fulfillment of the prophecy is connected one last time with events at the gate (7.17-20).[2] However, the emphasis in this last section is on the simultaneous fulfillment of the prophet's prediction of judgment on the king's captain. This connection is even reinforced with five occurrences of שער in these last four verses.[3] The last thing we are told is that the captain, who doubted God's ability to deliver, is trampled to death in the gate (שער). The gate which marks the way to salvation is also a place of judgment for the one who stands in the way.[4]

One last contrast might be drawn here. Whereas the deci-

than an expanding of the earlier phrase, makes its inclusion of שער even more noteworthy.

1 I follow Montgomery, *Kings*, p. 390, in reading שער here as the collective noun, 'gate-watch'.
2 LaBarbera, 'Man of War', pp. 650-51, notes these references to the gate and their significance.
3 The repetition of these verses and the possibility of textual corruption and/or redaction are discussed at length by Hobbs, *2 Kings*, pp. 87-88. The emphasis given here to the fulfillment of prediction is consonant with the agenda which von Rad stressed as being crucial to the framing of the Deuteronomistic History. See von Rad, 'The Deuteronomic Theology of History in I and II Kings', *The Problem of the Hexateuch and Other Essays* (trans. E.W. Trueman Dicken; London: Oliver & Boyd, 1966), pp. 208-12.
4 LaBarbera, 'Man of War', p. 651, helpfully points out how appropriate it is 'that the adjutant be dealt his just due in that place of justice, the gate, and by "the people"'.

2. The Stories in Literary-Aesthetic Perspective   103

sions of lepers had been instrumental in the saving of the city, the appointment (פקד) of the king is instrumental in the captain's death (7.17). In this story, life comes through unofficial channels, while the king's power is associated more and more with death—first in his threat to execute Elisha, next in his call to reject the lepers' report, and now finally in the fatal appointment of his captain to the gate. All of this stands out more clearly over against the king's opening words, 'How can I help (or "save", ישע) you, from the threshingfloor or from the winepress?' (6.27). As 1 Kgs 22.10 indicates, the threshingfloor of Samaria was at the gate. In the end the king was true to his word. The king, unlike Yahweh, could bring forth no salvation from the gate. He was, however, instrumental in bringing about the death of his captain there.[1]

Over against the contrast in the human means by which life and death are brought to the people of Israel, stands the common basis they share in the divine word. The story is intent on making this clear by placing the prophetic word at the story's center and then rehearsing it carefully at the very end. The action of this story is so fully turned over to people that the need is felt to remind everyone that these events are none other than the works of God.[2]

The story confirms the faithfulness of God's word and in so doing has something significant to say about human behavior. The behavior of the lofty is set over against the behavior of the lowly. The skeptical and negating actions of a king and his captain get them nowhere. The captain dies in the gate; the king is repeatedly trapped within the walls of his own isolation and paronoia. The commendable behavior of the lowly takes on an added significance insofar as it involves a subtle interfacing of divine and human initiative.[3] Through the exercise of mutual encouragement (7.3-4), shared conviction (7.9), and common sense (7.13) humble men unwittingly fulfill the salvation plans of God. Over against the king's opening question, 'If Yahweh will not help, how can I?', their actions show how

---

1 Ellul, *Politics of God*, p. 67, points also to the instrumental role of the mob in the captain's death.
2 The point remains whether or not this conclusion is ascribed to later redaction.
3 Cf. Ellul, *Politics of God*, pp. 630-72.

the Lord helps (and helps through) those who help one another.[1]

---

[1] I would note here that the king's opening question indicates a perceived dichotomy between God's help and his own help. The story, however, shows how the helping actions of the lepers merge with the saving action of God.

Chapter 3

THE THREE ELISHA STORIES IN CONTEXTUAL PERSPECTIVE

Introduction

The purpose of the present chapter is to relate what we have learned about the inner workings of each of our three Elisha stories to contextual considerations. It will be helpful to deal first with those contextual factors which have already been made relevant, either implicitly or explicitly, in past interpretations of these stories. This will give us a chance to pull together factors touched upon in the first chapter and test them further in the light of the foregoing literary-aesthetic analysis. This will also provide a good background for moving on to those contextual factors which have not been adequately appreciated in past treatment of our stories. These latter considerations will bring me to the full statement of my case for understanding these three narratives from the Elisha cycle as didactic salvation stories.

This treatment of contextual factors takes a broad and flexible view of context, seeing it in terms of various levels, including sociological, historical, ideological, and literary. Such an approach is in line with recent studies which have called for a more expanded and differentiated concept of 'setting' than the traditional concept of *Sitz im Leben* has provided.[1] It is neither my strategy nor my purpose here to attempt any systematic coverage of all possible matrices. I simply want to address

---

1 See Knierim, 'Form Criticism Reconsidered', pp. 463-66, and Douglas A. Knight, 'The Understanding of *Sitz im Leben* in Form Criticism', in *Society of Biblical Literature Seminar Papers 1974* (Missoula: Scholars, 1974), I, pp. 105-24.

those aspects of context to which earlier interpretations and my own encounter with these Elisha stories have pointed.

Prophetic Veneration

The background which has figured most prominently in past interpretation of the Elisha stories envisions a company of admiring followers united around a desire to venerate their prophetic hero. This view of the situation has attended the tradition of interpretation stemming from Hermann Gunkel. For Gunkel himself, as well as for most of the scholars who have followed him, this understanding of the generative context of the prophetical stories has not been an explicit focus of argument as much as an implicit assumption which has simply been taken for granted.

Gunkel's view of the context behind the prophetical narratives was firmly tied to his presuppositions as to how Israelite literature emerged. Gunkel saw the glorification of the national heroes as foundational not only for these and all other historical or hero sagas but also for the patriarchal sagas which he viewed as developmentally antecedent.[1] In his concern to trace the literary legacy of the entire Israelite people, Gunkel attributed this magnification of public heroes to the people at large and seems to have been unconcerned with identifying particularizations of this activity with specific times, places, or groups within Israelite society. The situation was no different in Gunkel's treatment of the legend,[2] which was to become the most important category in later treatments of the prophetical stories. Gunkel saw the intensification of the miraculous in the legend as especially reflective of the edificatory background.[3]

Despite the movement of later scholars away from Gunkel's developmental scheme, the same general edificatory background for these categories was carried forward in the terms themselves. With the expanding application of legend to the prophetical stories, which we traced earlier, together with

1 Gunkel, 'Sagen und Legenden', cols. 52-54; *Die israelitische Literatur*, pp. 19-21.
2 Gunkel, 'Sagen und Legenden', col. 58.
3 *Ibid.*

3. The Stories in Contextual Perspective 107

efforts to define legend more fully on the model of medieval Christian hagiology,[1] it became natural to view the edificatory background of these stories in more specific terms. With respect to the Elisha stories, this allowed edification to be located primarily among those of Elisha's own prophetical band.[2]

The latter view has found additional reinforcement from within the Elisha cycle by Elisha's repeated association with 'the sons of the prophets'.[3] Despite uncertainty about the precise nature and extent of this group,[4] clear indications of a posture of respect towards Elisha among its members[5] have understandably encouraged an identification with the hagiographical model. Special note has been taken, in this regard, of 2 Kgs 8.1-6, which records how one of Elisha's followers recounted, at the request of the king of Israel, 'all the great things that Elisha had done' (v. 4).[6] It is easy to see how this reference could be taken in support of a hagiographical background for the Elisha stories.

---

1 As indicated in Chapter 1, the authoritative formulation of this definition was set forth by Jolles, *Einfache Formen*, pp. 23-61.
2 For explicit statements of this assumption, see Tucker, *Form Criticism*, pp. 38-39; Gray, *Kings*, pp. 466-67. These examples are noted by Long, 'Social Setting', pp. 47-48. This assumption would seem to be implicit wherever the hagiographic model is indicated, e.g., Ellis, 'Kings', p. 198; Szikszai, 'Kings', p. 33; and Claus Westermann, *A Thousand Years and a Day: Our Time in the Old Testament* (trans. Stanley Rudman; Philadelphia: Fortress, 1962), p. 149.
3 Nine of the ten occurrences of this phrase appear in connection with Elisha: 2 Kgs 2.3, 5, 7, 15; 4.1, 38; 5.22; 6.1; 9.1. The one other occurrence is found just before the Elisha cycle in 1 Kgs 20.35.
4 A cautious review and assessment of the major views on this matter are given by J.R. Porter, 'בני־הנביאים', *JTS* ns 32 (1981), pp. 423-29.
5 Elisha's followers call him 'lord' (e.g., 2 Kgs 4.5, 15) and refer to themselves as his 'servants' (e.g. 2 Kgs 2.16; 4.1; 6.3). That Elisha's followers addressed him with the title 'father' has been argued by Phillips, 'The Ecstatics' Father', pp. 183-94; Williams, 'The Prophetic "Father"', pp. 344-48; on the analogy of the *'sons* of the prophets', however, Elisha is explicitly addressed by this title only by two Israelite kings (2 Kgs 6.2; 13.14). Still the posture of obedience and deference toward Elisha among 'the sons of the prophets' is clearly portrayed in their speech and actions. See, e.g., 6.1-3; 9.1-4.
6 See Sheldon Blank, *Understanding the Prophets* (New York: Union of American Hebrew Congregations, 1969), pp. 13-15.

The main point at issue here is the extent to which a hagiographic context corresponds to the internal dynamics and features which we have found in these three Elisha stories. With respect to 2 Kings 5, there are several prominent elements in the story which by themselves might seem indicative of an edificatory background, namely Elisha's power to heal a leper and curse a wicked servant, his authority over a foreign ruler, and his clairvoyance. However, the way these different things are situated and interrelated together with the other literary elements of the whole narrative indicates the questionableness of giving primacy to an edificatory background. We saw that the miracle of Naaman's healing is anticipated from the beginning of the story (v. 3). The impact of Elisha's power to do the impossible is thereby diffused from the outset.[1] Rather than accentuating Elisha's prowess as a wonder-worker, the narrative reflects some intent to play it down. By refusing the spotlight and any ostentatious display, which Naaman specifically expects, Elisha dissociates himself from the drama of the miracle.[2] This opens the way, as we saw, for the story to elevate the role of servants, both Naaman's and Elisha's, in bringing about the miracle. When Elisha refuses gifts from Naaman, his drawing back from the drama of the miracle is reinforced by his drawing back from the credit for it as well.

Understanding this story in terms of a hagiographic context is made dubious not only by how the story presents Naaman's healing but also by how the story points beyond it. Admittedly the way the story points beyond the miracle at one point could be taken as pointing precisely in the direction of venerating Elisha. We see this when Elisha calls for Naaman to come to him so that Naaman will 'know that there is a prophet in Israel' (v. 8). However, the same effect can be noted here that we noted in connection with the announcement of the little maid at the beginning of the story. Anticipating a solution to the given problem becomes a way for the narrative to move us on to a deeper issue. Thus, the issue of Naaman's healing, as presented by the little maid, gives way to the issue of

---

1 See Rofé, 'Classes', pp. 145-46.
2 See von Rad, 'Naaman', p. 50.

3. The Stories in Contextual Perspective 109

Naaman's acknowledgment of the prophet, as presented by Elisha, which in turn gives way to the issue which constitutes the actual crux of the narrative, submission before the God of Israel.

This deeper issue is reinforced by the symmetrical sequel which features Elisha's servant. Gehazi's downfall does not highlight what Elisha has done as much as what Naaman has done. Naaman's submission is sharply contrasted with Gehazi's lack of submission. Once again Elisha commands neither the foreground of dramatic action nor the center of dramatic tension. He has a decisive final word to both Naaman and Gehazi, but in each case it is a word which points beyond anything that he has done to the significance of what they have done.

A final point against the view that a hagiographical context stands behind this story might be that Gehazi's deed and the whole episode which records it would seem to be more of a debit than a credit to Elisha's reputation. One might also raise the question about how likely it would be for disciples bent on edifying their master to do so in a way that puts one of their own number in such a bad light.

Of these three Elisha stories, 2 Kgs 6.8-23 is perhaps the one most open to the claim of having originated from a hagiographic context. Elisha stands at the center of everything that happens. He knows what no one else knows and sees what no one else sees, and what he says controls all outcomes. Yet once again, when viewed within its full literary context, what Elisha does is seen to have a significance which is not to be confined to mere personal edification. Although Elisha's role is decisive, the final concern that is registered in both the introductory scene (vv. 8-10) and the developed episode (vv. 11-23) is not Elisha's position but rather the resulting relations between Aram and Israel. In fact, Elisha's actions in both instances defer finally to the action of Israel's king. Elisha's actions, then, are not presented as an end in themselves but rather as a catalyst for the complementary actions of others.

Reinforcing the latter point is the theme of vision. As we saw earlier, Elisha's role throughout the story centers on helping people to see. He informs the king of Israel to watch (שמר) with respect to the plotting Arameans (v. 9). He prays that his servant might see (ראה) the heavenly forces which surround them with protection (v. 17). After praying for the blindness of the Aramean army, Elisha prays for them to see (ראה) again, having taken them to Samaria (שמרון) before the eyes (note the verb ראה) of the king of Israel (vv. 20-21). One would expect a hagiographic context to manifest a concern to draw attention to Elisha, but the clear thrust of vision in this story is toward the unexpected forces which surround those who are now being given new sight. Moreover, Elisha's dependence upon prayer in bringing about this new sight might suggest a further qualification of the extent to which the story serves to draw attention to Elisha.

Our final story, 2 Kgs 6.24–7.20, is the least amenable of the three to claims for a hagiographic background. While Elisha's prophetic word stands forth boldly as the central pivot of the story, the actions of Elisha here, in contrast to what we saw in the earlier story, are decidedly defensive.[1] The scene of a vulnerable prophet seeking safety behind a locked door seems to be quite out of character with the hagiographic model.

We are pointed away from an edificatory context not only by what Elisha does but also by what he does not do in the story. As we saw in the last chapter, after the officer's question sharply poses the issue of how the deliverance predicted by Elisha could be accomplished, the story proceeds to develop and highlight the point that deliverance comes through the initiatives of servants and social outcasts. The prophet stays completely in the background as the story demonstrates how a network of humble human responses is orchestrated to accomplish God's will.[2] That God uses unexpected parties to fulfill his plans stands squarely at the heart of the story and squarely outside any narrow agenda of venerating the prophet Elisha.

The foregoing considerations are not intended to rule out the possible relevance of a hagiographic background for *all* of the Elisha stories. Other Elisha stories which have little to say beyond the actual recounting of the miracle would seem to be

1 See Hobbs, *2 Kings*, p. 81.
2 See Ellul, *Politics of God*, pp. 34, 67-70.

3. *The Stories in Contextual Perspective* 111

more open to being explained in terms of such a background.¹ Whatever might be said in favor of this possibility, and it is not my purpose here to pursue it, I have only attempted to show why these three particular stories should not be explained primarily in this way.

Prophetic Conflict

It will be helpful to turn next to a consideration of prophetic conflict as a background for the Elisha stories, since it lies closest to what we have just discussed. As we may recall from the previous discussion, Burke O. Long was the leading advocate for seeing the prophetical miracle stories against a background of prophecy's vindication rather than a prophet's veneration.² Long argued that whereas there is no concrete evidence for a cult of veneration in the Old Testament, there is abundant evidence for the prophetic conflict which would have generated apologetics for the prophetic institution.³ Reinforcing his argument with ethnographic parallels, Long identified such apologetics with the prophetic miracle stories. He later posited that these apologetics served not only the claims of the prophetic institution but also the prophetic claims of the individual.⁴ Although Long did not restrict the prophetic miracle stories to prophetic legitimation, he seems to suggest

1 2 Kgs 2.19-22; 2.23-24; 4.1-7; 4.38-41; 4.42-44; 6.1-7; 13.20-21. Rofé, 'Classification', p. 430, sets these narratives apart from the rest of the Elisha narratives as examples of the simple *legendum*. Cf. Long, 'Social Setting', p. 48.
2 Long, 'Social Setting', pp. 46-58. In taking this position Long went against his own earlier assumption that the miracle stories were edificatory. See 'Oracular Fulfillment Narrative', p. 199.
3 Long cites the comprehensive study of James L. Crenshaw, *Prophetic Conflict: Its Effect upon Israelite Religion* (BZAW 124; Berlin: de Gruyter, 1971). Other important studies on the subject include Gerhard von Rad, 'Die falschen Propheten', *ZAW* 51 (1933), pp. 109-20; G. Quell, *Wahre und falsche Propheten* (Gütersloh: Bertelsmann, 1952); F.L. Hossfeld and I. Meyer, *Prophet gegen Prophet: Eine Analyse der alttestamentlichen Texte zum Thema: Wahre und falsche Propheten* (Biblische Beiträge, 9; Fribourg: Schweizerisches Katholisches Bibelwerk, 1973); Robert P. Carroll, *When Prophecy Failed: Cognitive Dissonance in the Prophetic Traditions of the Old Testament* (New York: Seabury, 1979); DeVries, *Prophet Against Prophet*.
4 Long, 'Prophetic Authority', pp. 3-20.

that this was the primary background from which none of these stories was essentially independent.[1] This view was later explicitly argued by Thomas Overholt, who saw this background as the original context of the prophetic power acts themselves.[2] Simon DeVries, as our earlier discussion pointed out, also saw prophetic conflict as a dominant contextual matrix behind the prophetical narratives.[3] While he saw the different stories reflecting this matrix in different ways and in varying degrees, he recognized it as common to them all.[4] The three Elisha stories we have examined, we may recall, were clearly identified by DeVries against this background, with 2 Kings 5 being designated as a power-demonstration narrative and the other two narratives as prophet-authorization narratives.[5]

In identifying the miracle stories of Elisha with the context of prophetic legitimation, Long did not depend on any internal features of the stories other than their presentation of a prophetic miracle.[6] At one point Long even seized a chance to downplay the value of literary content to his argument:

> The fact that themes of hostility and disbelief are absent in the stories of 2 Kgs 2–7 need not count against my suggestion, since, if the ethnographical data are to be trusted, tales about shamans and their wondrous deeds likewise fail to mention directly the sociological situation in which they find their important function and setting.[7]

Several factors, however, argue against the lack of importance given to literary content in Long's argument. In the first place, it is clear that Long limited the relevance of literary content to his argument before having given it careful attention. This can be seen in relation to the above quotation. Whereas Long here claimed an absence of hostility and skepticism toward the prophet in 2 Kings 2–7, this collection's last story, which belongs to the group we have studied, features

---

1 Long, 'Social Setting', p. 48.
2 Overholt, 'Seeing is Believing', p. 23.
3 DeVries, *Prophet against Prophet*, p. viii.
4 *Op. cit.*, p. 73.
5 *Op. cit.*, pp. 53-55.
6 Long, 'Social Setting', p. 48.
7 *Op. cit.*, pp. 57-58.

3. The Stories in Contextual Perspective   113

bold examples of both, namely the Israelite king's death threat against Elisha (6.3) and the officer's skeptical response to Elisha's prediction of deliverance (7.2). Obviously prophetic legitimation is not the only contextual factor which could account for the recording of prophetic miracles.[1] Given this fact, taking full account of the content of these stories becomes extremely important.

Giving further support to the foregoing criticism, both DeVries and Overholt make specific appeal to literary content in their attempts to place the Elisha stories against a background of prophetic legitimation. DeVries's appeal is admittedly quite general and leaves comprehensive content analysis to later study.[2] Moreover, Overholt's analysis focuses narrowly on recorded responses to the prophet's miracles and does not intend to establish the background of the stories as much as the background of the prophetic acts of power themselves, although he does see the latter as having some bearing on the former.[3]

What is called for in response to these efforts to relate the Elisha stories to the background of prophetic legitimation is a consideration of the extent to which this context can be seen to correspond to the content we have observed in these three Elisha stories.[4] In pursuing this question, much of what was said earlier with respect to the stories' relation to prophetic veneration is relevant in much the same way. This is understandable, since there could hardly be a great deal of difference between elevating an individual by portraying his prophetic action and elevating prophetic action by portraying its execution by an individual.

The same prophetic feats which by themselves would seem to make the Naaman narrative amenable to an edificatory background could also be taken as evidence for prophetic apologetics. Several additional features of the story might even

---

1 Other possibilities would include those we shall take up next: polemics against Baal worship and class conflict.
2 DeVries, *Prophet against Prophet*, pp. 53, 56.
3 Overholt, 'Seeing is Believing', pp. 21-23.
4 We would expect a story to reveal its relevance to prophetic legitimation even where, granting Long's point, a situation of antagonism toward the prophet is not explicitly portrayed.

appear to reinforce this latter idea. In the little Hebrew maid's opening speech (5.3) reference is not made to Elisha's personal identity but rather only to his vocation as a prophet. This emphasis is especially noteworthy in view of the previously noted role of this speech in establishing the goal of the episode. The same emphasis is maintained at the crucial turning point of the story when Elisha calls for Naaman to come to him (5.8). It is not so that Naaman may know that Elisha heals leprosy that Elisha summons him, but rather so that Naaman 'may know that there is a prophet in Israel'. If it is easy to see how this statement could be taken to reflect a desire to draw attention to Elisha, a point considered earlier, then it should be even easier to see how it could be taken as reflective of a desire to vindicate prophecy.

If the foregoing features seem relevant to a background of apologetics for the prophetic vocation, then certain other features in the Naaman narrative might reflect the disfavor toward prophecy which such apologetics would have been reacting against. Most prominent among these would be Naaman's demonstrative resistance to Elisha's authority. As was pointed out in the earlier analysis, the narrative makes a special point of Naaman's initial unwillingness to approach the Israelite prophet with deference and respect (5.9-13). Drawing attention to how he had expected the prophet to act, Naaman's angry response indicates that a low regard for Elisha's prophetic status is at the root of his reaction. The responses of the Aramean and Israelite kings, though more subtle, might also reflect a less than positive attitude toward the prophet. Despite the Hebrew maid's explicit suggestion that Naaman go to the prophet, the Aramean king sends Naaman to the Israelite king with a letter which completely disregards the prophet (5.5-6). Just as the Aramean king ignores the prophet in writing the letter, the Israelite king ignores the prophet in reading the letter (5.7). Elisha's bold initiative toward the king of Israel in arranging an audience with Naaman suggests a move to break out of the unaccredited place which royal protocol had assigned to the prophet (5.8).

Notwithstanding all of the features which can be marshaled in support of placing the Naaman narrative against a back-

3. The Stories in Contextual Perspective   115

ground of prophetic apologetics, the full scope of the narrative, as disclosed in our literary-aesthetic examination, prevents one from making this background the primary one. The climax and consummation of the narrative clearly move beyond the concern to show 'that there is a prophet in Israel'. The focus upon Naaman's response to prophetic authority gives way after his healing to a focus upon his response to divine lordship, 'that there is no God in all the earth but in Israel' (5.15).[1] The key issue in this shift, as the strategic repetitions of נער, לפני, and עבד throughout the narrative make clear, is not so much the place of the prophet in Israel as the place of the servant in Israel. The Gehazi episode makes this abundantly clear. The complete narrative does not finally vindicate prophetic representatives over against antagonistic royal officials, as we would expect from prophetic apologetics. Rather the story draws the line elsewhere, between those who are willing to live as servants and those who refuse. As a result, salvation comes to a royal enemy, whereas judgment falls upon one from the prophet's own number.[2]

The other two Elisha stories which we have analyzed could be situated more easily within a context of prophetic apologetics. In each of these stories the prophet plays a central role in making known God's work in bringing about a dramatic deliverance. Yet a striking contrast in the way the two narratives portray the prophet should be acknowledged. In the ambush at Dothan Elisha openly faces an entire enemy army, whereas in the siege of Samaria he hides behind a locked door in response to the approaching footsteps of an Israelite messenger and king. If both of these narratives are to be located primarily against the background of prophetic legitimation,

1   Overholt, 'Seeing is Believing', p. 4, includes this verse among his examples of responses which register simple acceptance of the prophet's authenticity. That Overholt limits this response to this function raises doubts about attempting to assess these responses to prophetic miracles apart from appreciating their respective contexts in the stories.
2   The episode of Gehazi's dishonesty would seem to be even more at odds with a background of prophetic legitimation than personal veneration, for if Gehazi's bad actions are subversive to Elisha's image, they would be even more subversive to the image of prophetism, of which Gehazi is a prime representative in the story.

then such radically different ways of portraying the prophet would seem to call for some explanation. One might argue that these diverse portrayals offer a natural complement to one another, with one showing the prophet in power and the other showing the prophet in weakness; with one showing the prophet in a position of authority with his countrymen and king and the other showing the prophet in a position of rejection and ostracism; with one showing the prophet as the source of a spectacular saving vision and the other showing the prophet as the source of an unimaginable saving word. While such contrasts would be helpful in establishing the diversity of prophetic activity, they would seem to stand in some tension with a narrow concern for the recognizability of authentic prophecy. Moreover, such diverse relations between the people and the prophet as these contrasts entail would tend to put some strain on the assumption of a common background of prophetic vindication.

Perhaps the most significant tension between the two narratives and the context of prophetic legitimation involves the move in each story to put decisive stress not on how people are to respond to the prophet but rather on how people are to respond to each other. In the story of the Aramean attempt to capture Elisha, we saw how the prophet's actions climaxed in the enabling of Israelites and Arameans alike to see one another in a different light, thereby ending the earlier cycle of conflict which had dictated their relations. In the story of the Aramean siege there is no disputing the emphasis that is placed upon the officer's failure to acknowledge the prophet's authority in predicting deliverance.[1] Nevertheless, the climactic deliverance itself is brought about by the co-operative initiatives of the four lepers, who act outside of any knowledge of what the prophet had said. The contrast drawn between their mutually supportive actions and the socially destructive

---

1 This emphasis is seen in Elisha's prediction of judgment on the officer and its actualization as well as in the repetitious concluding comment which underscores the point that the prediction of judgment on the officer had come true (7.17-20). Thus the emphasis is embedded in the make-up of the narrative whether or not the concluding comment is partially or completely relegated to later redaction, as was discussed earlier.

actions going on within the city, as our earlier study revealed, dominates the action of the entire story. The weight thus falls not on the mere fact that the prophet's word comes true but rather on how the prophet's word comes true, in a way that features the true Israelite and not just the true prophet.

In summary, holistic treatment of the content of the Naaman narrative yields some strong arguments against seeing prophetic legitimation as its primary background. The other two Elisha stories analyzed show much more compatibility with such a background. Certain emphases in these stories, however, stand in some tension with a narrow idea of prophetic authorization. In view of these emphases, it would seem appropriate either to adopt a broader, more nuanced conception of prophetic apologetics than previous scholars have acknowledged or else consider the prospect that there is another matrix which shows a greater correspondence with the content of these stories.

Conflict With Baalism

Leah Bronner's work has stood alone among the major treatments of the Elisha materials in seeing Yahwism's conflict with Baalism as the primary background behind the Elisha stories.[1] As we observed in our earlier discussion, Bronner saw all of the Elijah and Elisha stories as 'deliberate polemics against Canaanite mythology'.[2] She developed her case, we may recall, by pointing up the threat of Baal worship in ninth-century Israel,[3] by pointing out the motifs associated

---

1 Bronner, *Stories of Elijah and Elisha*. See the discussion in Chapter 1.
2 *Op. cit.*, p. 139.
3 *Op. cit.*, pp. 8-17. Bronner's discussion here treats the period of Elijah and Elisha as a unity, oblivious to changes in the shape and scope of Baalism's threat throughout this time. Bronner assumes without question that this threat was as central during the time of Elisha as it was during Elijah's ministry, despite the fact that her discussion revolves entirely around Jezebel's conflict with Elijah. Bronner seems puzzled by Elisha's lenient attitude toward pagans in 2 Kgs 6.22 (p. 14), but the absence of any open clash with paganism in the Elisha stories, in contrast to the Elijah stories, is not even noticed. For more discriminating discussions, which appreciate the

with Baal's activity and dominion, as they appear in Ugaritic literature, and by pointing to instances where these motifs, or traces of them, appear in connection with Yahweh in the stories of Elijah and Elisha. Bronner assumed that the identification of Baal-associated motifs in the stories verified their polemical background. As was pointed out earlier, this reasoning disregarded the possibility that such motifs were not the controlling motifs of the stories; it also disregarded the possibility that the motifs in question may have served other intentions different from or in addition to any reference to Canaanite mythology. To have established her thesis against these possibilities would have required what Bronner called for but failed to provide—'a close study of the stories of Elijah and Elisha'.[1]

We can now test Bronner's thesis more closely with respect to the three Elisha stories which we have analyzed. For 2 Kings 5 Bronner identified divine healing, a prerogative of the gods in Ugaritic literature, as the polemic-constituting motif.[2] She saw an additional polemical touch in the Israelite king's anxious question ('Am I God to kill and make alive?'), which she viewed as an allusion to Baal's association with resurrection in Ugaritic mythology.[3] The polemical intention of these elements, as prescribed by Bronner, is made doubtful by several factors. First, both of these motifs are quite familiar in Yahwistic tradition,[4] and for that reason they are not espe-

---

dynamism of Yahwism's encounter with Baalism in this period and the presence of coexistent social, economic, and political currents, see John Bright, *A History of Israel* (3rd edn; Philadelphia: Westminster, 1981), pp. 240-51; Siegfried Herrmann, *A History of Israel in Old Testament Times* (trans. John Bowden; Philadelphia: Fortress, 1975), pp. 208-19; Yehezkel Kaufmann, *The Religion of Israel, From its Beginnings to the Babylonian Exile* (trans. Moshe Greenberg; New York: Schocken Books, 1972), pp. 273-82; J. Maxwell Miller and John H. Hayes, *A History of Ancient Israel and Judah* (Philadelphia: Westminster, 1986), pp. 250-302.

1 Bronner, *Stories of Elijah and Elisha*, p. 139.
2 *Op. cit.*, p. 104.
3 *Ibid.*
4 As noted by Hobbs (*2 Kings*, p. 64), these very motifs are used in Yahweh's self-description in Deut. 32.29: 'There is no god beside me; I kill and I make alive; I wound and I heal'. For a discussion of the

3. The Stories in Contextual Perspective 119

cially suggestive of Canaanite connections. Secondly, it is difficult to see how the king's rhetorical question in 5.7 could have served a polemical agenda, since the question registers the impotence of an Israelite, whose religious tradition in this instance would be giving him no advantage over a pagan worshiper. Thirdly, we saw in our earlier analysis that the king's question, by referring to God, serves the more obvious intention of setting the stage for the introduction of 'the man of God' in the next verse. The contrast, then, is not between Yahweh's claims and those of a rival but rather betwen the king ('Am I God?') and the prophet ('man of God').

The most significant problem with seeing Naaman's healing in terms of anti-Baal polemics is that the thrust of the episode, as our literary study has shown, does not culminate with Naaman's physical healing but rather with his becoming a servant before Elisha and his God. Moreover, the leniency of Elisha toward Naaman's future participation at the pagan temple is totally out of character with religious polemics. As the Gehazi episode more fully shows, the story is not so much concerned with the line between pagan and Israelite as with the line between servanthood and lording it over others.

The polemical parallel which Bronner identified for 2 Kgs 6.8-23 involves a contrast between the horses and chariots of fire and Baal's control of fire and lightning.[1] Once again, however, a full view of the surrounding literary features indicates that the story is here posing a contrast which is different from the one Bronner saw. The fiery horses and chariots surrounding Elisha, we recall, are set over against the Aramean horses and chariots surrounding Dothan, with clear and direct verbal echoes.[2] The story is indeed concerned that people catch a fresh vision of Yahweh's power, but the opposing power, both when the Arameans surround Elisha and when Samaria surrounds the Arameans, is not that of a divine rival but rather that of human militarism.

---

theme of divine healing and the cleansing of the leper in the Old Testament see, R.K. Harrison, 'Healing', *IDB*, II, pp. 541-46.
1 Bronner, *Stories of Elijah and Elisha*, p. 64.
2 In addition to the earlier discussion, see LaBarbera, 'Man of War', p. 641.

The story of the siege of Samaria has been seen as having more explicit allusions to pagan mythology than the others. Benhadad, the dynastic name of the Aramean king, has been taken as one such allusion.[1] With its reference to Hadad, the Aramean weather god and counterpart to Baal, the use of this name has been viewed as a subtle attempt to pit this deity against Yahweh. Bronner saw the central polemical motif of this story in the officer's skeptical response to Elisha's prediction of an imminent and abrupt end to the famine: 'If the Lord made windows in heaven, how could this thing be?' Bronner took this statement as a direct allusion to the windows of Baal's house, which refer in Ugaritic literature to the rain-producing clouds which Baal controlled.[2]

It must be argued, however, that a reference to Baal in the officer's words is not self-evident nor even likely. As was previously indicated, the Ugaritic tradition of rain from Baal's windows is not as relevant to a siege story and is not as appropriate for a Hebrew character or as likely for a Hebrew author as the Hebrew tradition of manna raining from heaven (Exod. 16.4). If our story had been written to challenge pagan claims of Baal's sovereignty over the processes of precipitation, as Bronner argued, then it is inconceivable that Yahweh would not be shown commanding those very forces of nature which Baal was thought to have controlled. Yet Yahweh succeeds by employing four lepers to recover the spoils of others. If our story represents Israelite polemic against Baalism, then surely it can be accused of backfiring, when Yahweh resorts to confiscating the produce of another. Yet the thrust of the story, as our detailed study has shown, centers not upon Yahweh's majestic control of nature *vis-à-vis* pagan claims but rather upon Yahweh's subtle action in history which delicately interfaces with humble human initiatives.

In summary, the foregoing observations would indicate that the concern to counter Baal worship has a very peripheral

---

1 So LaBarbera, 'Man of War', p. 646. LaBarbera does not see anti-Baal polemics as a primary background but rather a peripheral concern of the story. While his observation here strengthens Bronner's case, Bronner does not make this connection.
2 Bronner, *Stories of Elijah and Elisha*, p. 73.

place, if indeed it is present at all, in the background of these three Elisha stories.

Class Conflict

Whereas the recognition of socio-economic oppression within ninth-century Israel is not new,[1] only recently, in connection with the rise of interest in sociological approaches to Old Testament study,[2] has an argument been made for seeing peasant antipathy toward the ruling elite as the primary background of the Elisha stories. Robert LaBarbera's study of 2 Kgs 6.8– 7.20 offers the one clear statement of this view,[3] although there have been statements both before and since which have pointed in this direction in a more general way.[4]

Various references from the Elijah and Elisha stories suggest a picture of social and economic relations which could support this view. The Naboth narrative (1 Kgs 21) would be the most explicit depiction of economic exploitation of common Israelites by those in power. Also prominent would be the story of the Shunammite widow who appeals to Elisha to save her from losing her two sons to a creditor (2 Kgs 4). Other refer-

---

1 E.g. Julius Wellhausen, *Prolegomena to the History of Ancient Israel* (with a reprint of the article 'Israel' from the *Encyclopaedia Britannica*) (trans. J. Sutherland Black and Allan Menzies; Gloucester, Massachusetts: Peter Smith, 1973), p. 466. This work first appeared in the German in 1878.
2 See Robert R. Wilson, *Sociological Approaches to the Old Testament* (Philadelphia: Fortress, 1984); *Social Scientific Criticism of the Hebrew Bible and Its Social World: The Israelite Monarchy* (ed. Norman K. Gottwald; Semeia 37; Decatur, Georgia: Scholars, 1986); Bruce J. Malina, 'The Social Sciences and Biblical Interpretation', *Int* 37 (1982), pp. 229-42; Burke O. Long, 'The Social World of Ancient Israel', *Int* 37 (1982), pp. 243-55. The seminal studies in this vein have been George E. Mendenhall, *The Tenth Generation: The Origins of the Biblical Tradition* (Baltimore: Johns Hopkins University Press, 1973); Gottwald, *The Tribes of Yahweh: A Sociology of the Religion of Liberated Israel 1250–1050 B.C.E.* (Maryknoll, New York: Orbis, 1979); and Wilson, *Prophecy and Society in Ancient Israel* (Philadelphia: Fortress, 1980).
3 LaBarbera, 'Man of War'.
4 Prior to LaBarbera, see Brueggemann, *2 Kings*, pp. 1-6. Most recently, see Norman K. Gottwald, *The Hebrew Bible: A Socio-Literary Introduction* (Philadelphia: Fortress, 1985), pp. 351-52.

ences reflect situations of extreme poverty among those of the prophetic circles.[1] The same picture of socio-economic tensions is indirectly indicated by what is known of the policies and projects of the Omride dynasty.[2] The elaborate building programs of the Omrides[3] unquestionably point to massive amounts of conscripted labor and taxation.[4] The foreign trade relations established during this period appear to have followed the pattern of Solomon's time in bringing disproportionate concentrations of wealth to the urban centers, which the droughts of the time would have reinforced.[5] The resulting inequities do not implicate the Omrides alone, for the Jehu dynasty, despite its initial promises, appears by and large to have perpetuated this situation.[6]

The weight of LaBarbera's case for seeing 2 Kgs 6.8–7.20 against a background of peasant opposition toward a ruling elite rests primarily upon internal literary observations. We are thus on common ground with LaBarbera as we view his case in the light of the literary analyses presented in this study.

LaBarbera views 2 Kgs 6.8–7.20 as a composite of two stories which together form 'a cleverly constructed satire on the ruling elite of the day' by contrasting the successful actions of Elisha and other common folk with the complete ineptitude and impotence of 'kings, officials, and soldiers,... despite all their horses and chariots'.[7] A central support for LaBarbera's argument is the striking parallel he finds between two scenes

1 E.g. 2 Kgs 4.1; 5.22; 6.1-7.
2 For the most extensive treatment to date, see Stefan Timm, *Die Dynastie Omri: Quellen und Untersuchungen zur Geschichte Israels im 9. Jahrhundert vor Christus* (FRLANT, 124; Göttingen: Vandenhoeck & Ruprecht, 1982).
3 E.g. 1 Kgs 22.23 and 16.32.
4 For a discussion which includes relevant archaeological evidence, see Bright, *History*, pp. 242-45.
5 See H. Parzen, 'The Prophets and the Omri Dynasty', *HTR* 33 (1940), pp. 94-95.
6 This much is suggested by Amos' and Hosea's later perspective on the situation. See Bright, *History*, p. 253, and LaBarbera, 'Man of War', p. 638. The point here is especially significant for those who would follow Miller in dating the Elisha stories during the Jehu dynasty.
7 LaBarbera, 'Man of War', p. 637.

3. The Stories in Contextual Perspective

in the respective stories, both of which feature a king proposing what proves to be totally ineffective strategy as he consults with his servants. LaBarbera identifies the following scheme for 6.11-14 and 7.11-15:

1. The king consults his servant (עבדיו) about a military problem.
2. The king misunderstands the situation.
3. One of his servants (אחד מעבדיו) gives a pertinent suggestion.
4. The king sends (וישלח) chariots (רכב) and horses (סוסים) and commands his people to go and see (לכו וראו).[1]

In presenting these common elements, LaBarbera pays little attention to several significant differences: (1) the king of Aram is featured in the first scene, the king of Israel in the second, (2) the royal response in the first scene is offensive, that in the second is defensive, (3) in the first scene the king follows through with his miscalculated plan, in the second the king is talked out of his plan in favor of his servant's, (4) the first scene is primary to establishing the plot of the episode, the second plays a subsidiary role, coming after the climax and serving only to retard the resolution. If these differences raise some doubts about whether the given parallels reflect a deliberately repeated scheme, LaBarbera still seems to be on solid ground in seeing the impotence of officialdom as a prominent theme for both of these stories.

LaBarbera points to other literary features which reinforce the contrast between royal failure and the success of the uncredentialed. In the first story LaBarbera notes this contrast in relation to the language which describes Elisha and his actions. As we saw earlier, Elisha's initial advice to 'keep watch' (השמר) highlights Elisha's nullification of Aramean strategy by generating word rhyme with the secret location of the Arameans (שם ארם), the resolving announcement in v. 10 that Israel was thus repeatedly preserved (נשמר), and Elisha's final triumph over the Arameans in Samaria (שמרון).[2] LaBarbera further suggests, we may recall, that the sym-

---

1 *Op. cit.*, p. 650.
2 *Op. cit.*, pp. 640 and 644.

metrical contrast drawn between the heavenly forces and the Aramean (vv. 15-17) includes no heavenly counterpart to the Aramean army (חיל) if it is not Elisha himself.[1] If LaBarbera overstates Elisha's role in claiming him as the commander of the heavenly forces,[2] he is on firmer ground in appreciating the way the narrative highlights Elisha's takeover of Aramean command by placing in Elisha's mouth the imperatives earlier issued by the king of Aram ('go and see').[3] Elisha's concluding role in controlling the Israelite king's action is seen by LaBarbera to complete the foregoing pattern: 'Elisha completely outmaneuvers the military establishments of the day on both sides'.[4]

LaBarbera sees the same caricaturing of royal power in the second story, even though Israelite rather than Aramean power is here the focus. He views the king's exasperated response to the woman's cry for help in the opening scene as the key to the scene's primary function of showing 'the ineffectiveness of the Israelite king'.[5] Over against the king's admission of impotence stands the forcefulness of Elisha's saving word. Yet LaBarbera finds an even more significant statement of the contrast in the depiction of the lepers. Through word play, the introduction of the four (ארבעה) lepers suggests an immediate counterpoint to the officer's skeptical question as to how such deliverance could come, even if Yahweh made windows (ארבות) in heaven.[6] The officer's words represent royal impotence, thinks LaBarbera, and their punishment marks the end of the story. The actions of these lepers by contrast prove to be the chief delivering force in the story. LaBarbera finds word play used again to punctuate the lepers'

---

1 *Op. cit.*, p. 641.
2 Elisha's depiction as heavenly commander is made less likely by the emphasis on Elisha's recourse to prayer in the passage.
3 *Op. cit.*, p. 643. The second Aramean imperative is not reissued in the form of an imperative by Elisha but rather it is taken up in a prayer to Yahweh that the Arameans might 'see'. This fact may suggest that, whereas LaBarbera stresses only Elisha's role *vis-à-vis* the Aramean king, more may need to be said for the narrative's emphasis upon Yahweh's role *vis-à-vis* the Aramean king.
4 *Op. cit.*, pp. 644-45.
5 *Op. cit.*, p. 647.
6 *Op. cit.*, p. 648.

3. *The Stories in Contextual Perspective* 125

reversal of role when the Arameans mistake the approaching lepers (מצרעים) for kings of Egypt (מצרים).[1] LaBarbera suggests that the contrast between the powerful and the powerless is reinforced throughout by the motif of 'the gate, that place where the world of the peasant met the world of the ruling elite'.[2]

LaBarbera's literary observations on the stories in 2 Kgs 6.8–7.20 make a strong case for seeing 'their ultimate source in a peasant milieu'.[3] The literary-aesthetic study presented above has corroborated many of these insights and offered others which could well serve LaBarbera's case. In the first story, LaBarbera's contrast between Elisha and 'the military establishment of both sides' could be reinforced by our earlier observations of the way Elisha's actions are structurally and thematically situated between those of the two opposing kings. Both in the introductory scene (6.8-10) and in the larger episode (6.11-23), the initiative of Elisha is raised above those on either side by cancelling the preceding initiative of Aram's king and by directing the following initiative of the king of Israel. Similarly in our study of the second story we saw several literary features which could enhance the contrast LaBarbera draws between the lepers and those in power. We noted that there is a structural balancing of the destructive action of the king inside the city in the story's first movement with the life-saving action of the lepers outside the city in the story's second movement. In each case the specific action carries out the implications of an initial question ('How can I help?' vs 'Why should we sit here until we die?'). Both parties, we noted, generate the respective turning points of the two movements by declaring their contrasting intentions for the given 'day' (יום). The king decides death for the prophet, whereas the lepers decide on sharing 'good news' with the king and the city. Moreover, an additional contrast was noted in the fact that whereas the lepers bring salvation to the gate, the place where the threshingfloor was located[4] and the very place where Elisha said salvation would be fulfilled, the king

---

1 *Op. cit.*, p. 649.
2 *Op. cit.*, p. 651.
3 *Op. cit.*, p. 637.
4 See 1 Kgs 22.10.

ironically fulfills his own disclaimer of providing help from the threshingfloor by helping to bring about the death of his officer there.

Despite all the literary features in these stories which seem to correspond to a background of peasant antipathy toward those in power, our earlier study has noted other features which do not fit so well. The most notable such feature in the first story is Elisha's exceedingly positive relations with the king of Israel. Not only does Elisha show support and deference to the king in relation to the Aramean threat, but the king shows obvious respect for Elisha as well, as when he addresses the prophet as 'my father' (6.21). Robert Wilson consequently has argued that this narrative represents Elisha not as a 'peripheral prophet' but rather as one who stood 'closer to the political establishment and took on social maintenance functions'.[1] The soiciological terms of Wilson's assessment only highlight the problem of placing this story against an anti-establishment background. Elisha's actions in this story exhibit affirmation toward the establishment. A certain respect even for Aramean structures of authority is suggested by his advice to have the Aramean captives sent back to 'their lord' (6.22).

Certain features of the second story likewise seem to stand outside an anti-establishment agenda. The king and his officer are not the only characters to be depicted unfavorably over against the prophet and the lepers. As our earlier study pointed out, the common people in the city are also compared adversely with the lepers. The woman who decides to hide her son after helping to eat her friend's son contrasts with the lepers in their decision to refrain from hiding their life-saving plunder from the city. A more indirect indictment against the people in the city is the reference to the extortionate prices being exacted for the least morsel (6.25). We should note that the narrative does not implicate the king in this exploitation but rather suggests by the reference to his sackcloth (6.30)

---

[1] Wilson, *Prophecy and Society*, pp. 205-206. Wilson argues here that prior to Jehu's revolt Elisha was a peripheral prophet. Accordingly, he places this story during the Jehu dynasty. See Miller, 'Elisha Cycle'.

that he stands in solemn opposition to it. All of this seems out of character with a class-conscious agenda.

In short, both of these stories resist the kind of class stereotyping that LaBarbera's argument suggests. Royalty is not everywhere set over against the peasantry, as we can see from the king's close relations with Elisha in the first story and his sackcloth in the second. The characterization of commoners is similarly diversified to include the siege victims' vicious exploitation of one another in the first story and the initial impotence and fear of Elisha's servant in the second.

Turning to the Naaman narrative, which LaBarbera's study does not specifically treat, the latter argument applies in even greater measure. This story, as we noted, certainly follows the others in illustrating the inability of the ruling establishment, both Aramean and Israelite, to bring deliverance. However, the central thrust of the whole story directly reverses the pattern of the commoner coming out on top over the aristocrat, for the Aramean ruler attains healing whereas the Israelite servant is punished with leprosy. If anything, this story would serve to counter an anti-establishment tendency.

Perhaps one could argue that despite the role reversal of the actual servant and lord portrayed in the story, the central affirmation of servanthood over lordship still indicates an anti-establishment agenda. But how anti-establishment (in the normal socio-economic sense) could this story's affirmation of servanthood be when special allowance is made for Naaman to keep a privileged social position, while special repudiation is registered for Gehazi's economic interests? The Naaman story rather seems to be affirming servanthood at a theological level which forcefully addresses but ultimately transcends class struggle. If anything, this story would serve to counter an anti-establishment agenda.

In summary, there are a good number of elements in these three Elisha stories which suggest a context of class resistance toward the ruling elite. However, we saw that a clear line between the classes is not consistently maintained throughout the stories, and in the Naaman narrative the sides are even inverted. This suggests that while social tensions may well inform these stories, the primary line being drawn and the primary background being represented is to be found elsewhere.

Theological Struggle with Aramean Domination

In the light of the questions raised with respect to the foregoing views, we come now to a view of the background of the given Elisha stories which has been surprisingly neglected. This view sees the primary background of these stories in the efforts by loyal Yahwists to identify and explicate the saving action of Yahweh at a time when Aram's sustained military threat against Israel placed a question mark over Yahweh's role as Israel's deliverer. Even before we consider the internal testimony of these stories, the viability of this background is suggested by the convergence of two lines of evidence which range beyond these stories. One concerns the prominence and shape of the Aramean military threat in ninth-century Israel; the other concerns the prominence and specific handling of traditional salvation motifs in the wider literary context. We shall look at these factors separately before viewing their convergence.

There is no disputing the fact that Aramean militarism ranks alongside the lure of pagan worship as one of the two greatest threats faced by ninth-century Israel.[1] As was the case with our perspective on Israel's encounter with Baalism, there is some uncertainty about the full historical course of the Aramean threat throughout this period. Two basic views have emerged. One view, following the biblical chronology, sees continual Aramean aggressions extending from Ahab of the Omride dynasty to Jehoash of the Jehu dynasty. This view requires seeing these aggressions as part of a more fluctuating state of affairs in the Omride period before bringing about in the Jehu period a situation of sustained Aramean domination until Jehoash.[2] The other view envisages a more orderly course of events by restricting all Aramean warfare against

---

1 See Alan W. Jenks, *The Elohist and North Israelite Traditions* (SBLMS, 22; Missoula: Scholars, 1977), pp. 95-96.
2 Proponents of this view include Bright, *History*, pp. 242-43, 253-55; Kaufmann, *Religion of Israel*, pp. 277-82; Herrmann, *History*, pp. 213-14.

3. The Stories in Contextual Perspective 129

Israel to the Jehu period, thus viewing biblical references to such warfare in the Omride period as anachronisms.[1] The limitations of the sources at this point make a definitive reconstruction impossible.[2] Nevertheless, Aramean militarism is seen to be the primary and persistent external threat against Israel in the period in which our three Elisha stories, in either case, would be placed.[3]

A second line of evidence supporting the proposed background involves the appearance of several prominent salvation motifs in the Elisha cycle which would seem to accord with a context of theological deliberation on traditional notions of salvation. Most prominent of all, perhaps, is Elisha's repeated association with horses and chariots. As a crowning appellation at the close of the prophet's life, King Joash refers to Elisha as 'the chariots of Israel and its horsemen' (2 Kgs 13.14). Similarly, in the story which records the beginning of Elisha's ministry, Elisha applies this same appellation to Elijah when the two are dramatically parted from one another by 'a chariot and horses of fire' (2 Kgs 2.11-12). Insofar as this latter story seems to belong to the Elisha cycle, Elijah here may have 'inherited' the given epithet from his successor rather than vice versa.[4] While Elisha's description as 'the chariots and horsemen of Israel' has been given some abstruse connections,[5] the obvious significance of the epithet is that it is Israel's

---

1 A strenuous argument for this view has been put forward by J. Maxwell Miller, 'The Elisha Cycle and the Accounts of the Omride Wars', *JBL* 85 (1966), pp. 441-54. For a clear summation of the argument, see Miller and Hayes, *History*, pp. 252, 262, 297-302.
2 A fair acknowledgment of the uncertainty is registered by Herbert Donner, 'The Separate States of Israel and Judah', ch. 7 in *Israelite and Judean History*, ed. John H. Hayes and J. Maxwell Miller (Philadelphia: Westminster, 1977), pp. 399-400. See also the cautious comments of Norman K. Gottwald, *All the Kingdoms of the Earth: Israelite Prophecy and International Relations in the Ancient Near East* (New York: Harper & Row, 1964), pp. 84-85.
3 The three stories which we have studied, insofar as they are given no specific chronological identification, are easily shifted to the Jehu period for those following the latter view.
4 The case is clearly made by Hermann Gunkel, 'Elisha, the Successor of Elijah (2 Kings ii.1-18)', *ExpTim* 41 (1929-1930), pp. 182-86.
5 Galling, 'Der Ehrenname Elisas und die Entrückung Elias', *ZTK* 53 (1956), p. 148, sees intentional contrast with the name of the

prophet, not its conventional military resources, that represents the true strength and salvation of the nation in its confrontation with foreign military aggression.[1] Accordingly, Elisha is shown playing a decisive charismatic role in Israel's warfare, not only in the narratives we have examined but also in the stories of Joash's clash with the Arameans (2 Kgs 13.14-19) and Jehoram's battle against Moab (3.1-27).

To gain some needed perspective on Elisha's relation to warfare and on the more specific nature of the salvation motifs of the Elisha cycle, it is important that we look at three different ways in which the war motifs of the Elisha stories can be related to a wider Israelite tradition. These three ways correspond to traditio-historical work done on the following three areas: early Israelite prophecy, holy war, and exodus-conquest traditions.

One plausible way of situating the war motifs of the Elisha cycle is suggested by the view that sees warfare as a constitutive ingredient either of early Israelite prophecy or of one of its dominant strains. Without disregarding the meagerness of available evidence on the origins of Israelite prophecy,[2] several scholars have supported such a view.[3] This view would see the

Aramean war-god, רכבאל. Georg Fohrer, *Elia* (2nd edn; ATANT, 53; Zürich: Zwingli, 1968), p. 100, suggests that the epithet implies the prophet's promotion to God's heavenly army where his struggle can continue.

1 Among the overwhelming majority who take this view are Gunkel, 'Elisha', pp. 184-85; Burney, *Notes*, p. 265; Montgomery, *Kings*, p. 354; Gray, *Kings*, p. 476; M.A. Beek, 'The Meaning of the Expression "The Chariots and the Horsemen of Israel" (II Kings ii 12)', *OTS* 17 (1972), pp. 3-4; von Rad, *Heilige Krieg*, p. 55.

2 For a recent and discerning review of this area see J.R. Porter, 'The Origins of Prophecy in Israel', in *Israel's Prophetic Tradition: Essays in Honour of Peter Ackroyd* (ed. Richard Coggins, Anthony Phillips, and Michael Knibb; Cambridge: Cambridge University Press, 1982), pp. 12-31.

3 Principal advocates are Martin Buber, *Königtum Gottes* (3rd edn; Heidelberg: L. Schneider, 1956), p. 142; Rolf Rendtorff, 'Reflections on the Early History of Prophecy in Israel' (trans. Paul J. Achtemeier), *JTC* 4 (1967), pp. 14-34; and, more recently, Joseph Blenkinsopp, *A History of Prophecy in Israel: From the Settlement in the Land to the Hellenistic Period* (Philadelphia: Westminster, 1983), pp. 59-79, who sees 'a type of war prophecy' as the primary, if not the only, strain in the emergence of Israelite prophecy. All of these

prophet's role in warfare, as presented in the Elisha cycle, as simply an extension of this early conjunction between warfare and prophetic activity. Along these lines, it would be difficult to see the war motifs of the Elisha cycle as reflecting anything less than a central concern of ninth-century prophecy.

While the foregoing view of connecting warfare to the origins of Israelite prophecy has been challenged on the basis of insufficient evidence,[1] some of the leading exponents of this view have nevertheless reinforced the strong connection between warfare and prophecy in ninth-century Israel.[2] Their line of argument opens up the second way of relating the war motifs of the Elisha cycle to a wider Israelite tradition. The focus here is not on how warfare relates to the history of Israelite prophecy but rather on how prophecy relates to the history of Yahwistic warfare.

At the center of this latter discussion stands Gerhard von Rad's diachronic reconstruction of the tradition of holy war in

    scholars arrive at this view on the basis of loose connections and associative links between early warfare practices and prophetic activity. Offering additional and distinctive support to this view is Robert Bach, *Die Aufforderungen zur Flucht und zum Kampf im alttestamentlichen Prophetenspruch* (WMANT, 9; Neukirchen: Neukirchener Verlag, 1962), pp. 92-112, who attempts to push the connection between prophecy and warfare back to the earliest period of Israelite prophecy on the basis of form-critical links between the earliest appearances of the summons to battle and later prophetic speech.
1 So von Rad, *Heilige Krieg*, p. 54; Rudolf Smend, *Yahweh War and Tribal Confederation: Reflections upon Israel's Earliest History* (trans. Max Gray Rogers; Nashville: Abingdon, 1970), pp. 73-74; Patrick D. Miller, 'The Divine Council and the Prophetic Call to War', *VT* 18 (1968), pp. 105-106; and his *The Divine Warrior in Early Israel* (HSM, 5; Cambridge, MA: Harvard University, 1973), pp. 133-35. However, more recently such challenges have been answered with the impressive article of James S. Ackerman, 'Prophecy and Warfare in Early Israel: A Study of the Deborah-Barak Story', *BASOR* 220 (1975), pp. 5-15. Building upon Bach's form-critical approach with reinforcement from comparative evidence from Mari and other ancient Near Eastern sources, Ackerman offers a fresh argument for the inherent union of warfare and prophecy in pre-monarchical Israel.
2 See von Rad, *Heilige Krieg*, pp. 54-56; *idem*, *Old Testament Theology*, vol. 2 (trans. D.M.G. Stalker; New York: Harper & Row, 1965), p. 29; Miller, 'Divine Council', pp. 106-107.

ancient Israel.¹ Von Rad proposed that a discretely identifiable model of holy war, rooted in pre-Solomonic cultic institutions, offered a basis for identifying all later developments and their place in a complete history of Israel's theology of warfare. This classic holy-war schema was defined in terms of a series of major elements: (1) the mustering of a voluntary army, (2) adherence to sacral orders, including sexual abstinence, (3) the solicitation of a favorable oracle, (4) formalized exhortations to faith and assurances of divine presence before the enemy, (5) divine terror upon the enemy camp before the victory shout of Israel, (6) the ensuing fight, which gives chief, if not exclusive, place to Yahweh's power, (7) the ḥerem-sacrifice of all spoils to Yahweh, and (8) the dispersion announcement 'to your tents, O Israel'.²

The connections between this proposed holy-war tradition and the war materials of the Elisha cycle are easy to see. We might first recognize the connections which stand forth from the narratives we have previously examined. In the story of Elisha's ambush by the Aramean army, Elisha's words of reassurance to his alarmed servant, 'Fear not, for those who are with us are more than those who are with them' (2 Kgs 6.16), can be identified with the language and function of the holy-war call to faith. Indeed, von Rad identified 'Fear not!' as a standard holy-war expression.³ The ensuing deliverance of Elisha and his servant features what would have to be considered the holy-war tradition's most essential characteristic—the saving miracle of Yahweh, manifested here in the spectacle of horses and chariots of fire and the blinding of the Aramean army (6.17-18). Yahweh's miraculous power also plays the decisive role in the story of the Aramean siege of Samaria, when the Aramean camp is made to 'hear the sound of chariots and horses and a great army' (7.6). The Arameans' 'flight in the twilight' points up yet another feature of the given holy-war schema—the sudden panic of the enemy camp at the sound of the approaching army.

1 A helpful summary of von Rad's *Heilige Krieg* is presented by James L. Crenshaw, *Gerhard von Rad* (Makers of the Modern Theological Mind; Waco, TX: Word Books, 1978), pp. 42-52.
2 Von Rad, *Heilige Krieg*, pp. 6-14.
3 *Op. cit.*, pp. 9-10.

3. The Stories in Contextual Perspective 133

Other parallels with this holy-war schema can be drawn elsewhere in the Elisha cycle. In the war with the Moabites, success is not experienced until a favorable oracle is secured from the prophet Elisha (2 Kgs 3.9-19). The oracle makes use of what is for von Rad a standard holy-war formula: 'Yahweh has given (the enemy) into your hand' (3.18).[1] Then comes the dramatic Israelite victory, which turns, here again, on an enemy-confounding miracle performed by Yahweh (3.17-24). A strong relation to the holy-war tradition has been claimed for the story of Jehu's blood purge of the house of Ahab (2 Kgs 9–10),[2] presumably insofar as it fulfills a divinely willed judgment (10.30) and proceeds from a prophetic commissioning (9.6-10). However, discrete elements of the classic schema are absent here, unless the prophetic commissioning be taken as having some connection to the battle oracle. A more tenable connection to the battle oracle can be seen in the final Elisha narrative, where Elisha has King Joash shoot an arrow and strike the ground to determine the extent of Israel's future military success against Aram (2 Kgs 13.14-19).

If we look beyond the Elisha cycle to other narratives of ninth-century prophecy, several other clear correspondences with the holy-war schema can be noted. The story of Ahab's victory over Benhadad in 1 Kings 20 features the standardized oracular assurance that Yahweh would 'give (the enemy) into your hand' (v. 13), a mustering of 'all the people of Israel' (v. 15), and a prophetic invoking of the holy-war ban (vv. 35-43). The Micaiah narrative in 1 Kings 22 offers an extended example of the solicitation of a pre-battle oracle (vv. 5-23). The royal decision to 'inquire first for the word of Yahweh' (v. 5) yields the standard words of prophetic assurance, 'Yahweh will give it [Aramean-occupied territory] into the king's hand' (vv. 6, 12, 15), though Micaiah speaks this oracle only to make mockery of it.[3] One could also see an element of the holy-war tradition in the story of Ahaziah's attempt to seize Elijah in 1 Kings 1. The 'fire of God' (vv. 10, 12, 14), which repeatedly

---
1 *Op. cit.*, pp. 7-8.
2 Jenks, *Elohist*, p. 97.
3 Miller, 'Divine Council', pp. 101-107, develops an argument that might also link the divine council of Micaiah's vision (1 Kgs 22.19) with the fundamental elements of the holy-war tradition.

protects Elijah by consuming Ahaziah's messengers, suggests itself as a prime example of the saving miracle which stands at the heart of the holy-war pattern.

Holy-war motifs in the pre-classical prophetical narratives, such as these we have just itemized, served to convince von Rad that the prophets of ninth-century Israel were, in actuality, primary representatives of the holy-war tradition. Von Rad saw the prophetic appellative, 'My father, my father, the chariots of Israel and its horsemen', as an important indicator of this, for the title, 'my father', he reasoned, could only have originated in the actual prophetical circles, who must have been registering in the complete title their understanding of the prophet's role at the time.[1]

Von Rad saw an even deeper significance in the appellation and so proposed a further insight into the prophetic ethos which he saw lying behind it. The identification of the prophet as the chariots and horsemen of Israel struck von Rad as a highly polemical term, suggestive of a vigorous prophetic opposition toward the monarchy's 'technologization' of the war process.[2] Von Rad saw the northern prophets as coming to take up this crusade rather naturally by way of their traditional involvement in the realm of politics.[3] Yet this promulgation of the holy-war tradition represented for von Rad a secondary taking up of an ancient tradition—a tradition now rescued from extinction by a prophetic movement from which it was originally independent.[4]

The essential point here for us is that, although von Rad rejected the generic link between Israelite prophecy and holy war, he offered another, perhaps even more forceful, way of identifying the agenda of warfare at the very center of ninth-century prophecy. Concern over the issue of warfare was not so much an inherent responsibility for the ninth-century prophets as a fresh and bold response to the exigencies of the time.

1 Von Rad, *Heilige Krieg*, pp. 54-56.
2 *Ibid*. In 1 Kgs 20 von Rad found clear testimony to this conflict between prophet and king over warfare.
3 *Op. cit.*, pp. 53-54.
4 *Ibid*.

3. The Stories in Contextual Perspective 135

Having found, primarily through von Rad's work, a second way of seeing the salvation motifs of the Elisha cycle within a broader perspective, we must now say something about the reliability of our find. Von Rad's diachronic reconstruction of holy war in Israel has been shown to be vulnerable at several points. We see this with von Rad's hypothesis of a 'Solomonic Enlightenment', his view that a revolutionary cultural shift took place during the time of Solomon, moving Israel from a completely sacral to a predominantly secular orientation.[1] This hypothesis, which so heavily informed the way von Rad dated and differentiated the texts and traditions with which he worked, has been shown to rest upon a very tenuous base.[2] If von Rad's view of the pan-sacral character of pre-monarchical Israel is in doubt, even more so is the more specific cultic context which he accepted as the original source of the holy-war tradition, namely, the tribal amphictyony.[3] The credibility of any application of the amphictyonic model to pre-monarchical Israel has been seriously undermined from several directions.[4] With the cultic base of von Rad's reconstruction of holy war in such doubt, an increasing number of scholars have called for abandoning the term 'holy war' in favor of the more neutral and biblically derived term 'Yahweh war'.[5] But

1 *Op. cit.*, pp. 39-42.
2 See James L. Crenshaw, *Old Testament Wisdom: An Introduction* (Atlanta: John Knox, 1981), pp. 42-54. See also his 'Prolegomenon', in *Studies in Ancient Israelite Wisdom* (ed. J.L. Crenshaw; New York: KTAV, 1976), pp. 16-20; and his review of *Wisdom in Israel*, by Gerhard von Rad, in *RSR* 2 (1976), pp. 6-12.
3 The theory that Israel began as a league of tribes bound together around a shared shrine on the Greek amphictyonic model was advanced by Martin Noth, *Das System der zwölf Stämme Israels* (BWANT, IV/1; Stuttgart: W. Kohlhammer, 1930). Von Rad accepted this theory without argument.
4 A presentation of the principal objections and objectors is given by Georg Fohrer, 'Altes Testament: "Amphiktyonie" und "Bund"?', *TLZ* 111 (1966), cols. 802-16, 893-904.
5 Smend, *Yahweh War*, p. 38; Wolfgang Richter, *Traditionsgeschichtliche Untersuchungen zum Richterbuch* (Bonn: P. Hanstein, 1963), p. 186; Helga Weippert, 'Jahwekrieg und Bundesfluch in Jer 21.1-7', *ZAW* 82 (1970), p. 396; Manfred Weippert, '"Heiliger Krieg" in Israel und Assyrien: Kritische Anmerkungen zu Gerhard von Rads Konzept des Heiligen Krieges im alten Israel', *ZAW* 84 (1972), pp. 490-91; Gwilym H. Jones, '"Holy War" or

the relinquishment of von Rad's terminology reflects more than just this. Scholars have shown increasing resistance to the idea that Israel's traditions of warfare can be traced back to some pure, established formula, such as von Rad set forth.[1]

Even when we grant the force of the foregoing criticism, the essential value of von Rad's work for illuminating the background of the Elisha stories is not significantly diminished. While substantial doubts are raised about the claims for a rigid, pristine pattern of holy war and its precise contexts and stages of development, it remains clear that the formulas and motifs identified by von Rad do indeed reflect a rich and forceful tradition among the Hebrews that Yahweh was vitally active in their warfare. And there appears no reason to doubt that the ninth-century prophets were intensely occupied with defending this general tradition in the way von Rad himself described.[2] This general tradition and not so much some specific configuration of its elements would seem to represent what was essentially at stake for the prophets of this time. Our inability to establish a more specific tradition, defined in terms of some pristine pattern, would not appear significantly to affect our view of what was going on here.

In contrast to von Rad's elusive pristine paradigm, there is another specific tradition which would seem to offer much more solid claims for standing behind and shedding additional light upon the war traditions of the ninth-century prophets. I refer here to the exodus–conquest tradition, which brings us

---

"Yahweh War"?', *VT* 25 (1975), pp. 642-58; Peter C. Craigie, *The Problem of War in the Old Testament* (Grand Rapids: Eerdmans, 1978), pp. 49-50.

1 The questionableness of von Rad's methodology here is succinctly stated by Crenshaw, *Gerhard von Rad*, pp. 42-45. See also Georg Fohrer, *Geschichte der israelitischen Religion* (Berlin: de Gruyter, 1969), p. 109; Richter, *Traditionsgeschichtliche Untersuchungen*, pp. 112-245; Norman K. Gottwald, 'War, Holy', *IDBSup*, pp. 942-44; Jones, '"Holy War"', pp. 648-55.

2 In the narratives we have reviewed, the testimony for connecting the prophets with warfare in this way could not easily be explained in terms of Deuteronomistic redaction, for, as Wilson, *Prophecy and Society*, p. 167, has pointed out, Deuteronomy's laws on prophetic activity in ch. 18 and on the conduct of warfare in ch. 20 show nothing of this connection.

finally to the third way of identifying the salvation motifs of the Elisha cycle within a larger perspective.

Recently, Millard C. Lind has made a substantial case for seeing the exodus event as the foundational and continuing paradigm for warfare in the Old Testament.[1] Evidence for the early date of the Song of the Sea,[2] supportive connections from Israel's ancient covenant forms as compared to second-millennium treaty structure,[3] and a convergence of testimony in the narrative accounts of the sea event[4] are brought together in support of the exodus event's foundational place. References to the conquest in the Song of the Sea, as well as the conquest narratives themselves, are seen to show how the exodus pattern emerged as the paradigm for Israel's subsequent military experiences.[5] Lind believes that this paradigm continued to have an imposing influence upon Israel's theology of warfare in every period, and his full study[6] carries this thesis through the Torah and Former Prophets.

As concerns the prophetical narratives, with which we are chiefly concerned, Lind finds the indirect influence of the exodus tradition in the instances of prophetic opposition toward the northern kings as they are shown conforming more and more to the contrasting Near Eastern concepts of warfare and

1 Millard C. Lind, 'Paradigm of Holy War in the Old Testament', *BR* 16 (1971), pp. 16-31; and also his *Yahweh is a Warrior: The Theology of Warfare in Ancient Israel* (Scottdale, Pennsylvania: Herald Press, 1980).
2 Lind appeals to the work of Frank M. Cross and David N. Freedman, 'The Song of Miriam', *JNES* 14 (1955), pp. 237-50; Cross, 'The Song of the Sea and Canaanite Myth', *JTC* 5 (1968), pp. 1-25; and David A. Robertson, *Linguistic Evidence in Dating Early Hebrew Poetry* (SBLDS, 3; Missoula, Montana: Society of Biblical Literature, 1972).
3 Lind, 'Paradigm', pp. 25-26, argues here that Israel's early covenant forms reflect the exodus paradigm by giving primacy to Yahweh's role in Israel's deliverance and by keeping these military references in the historical prologue sections, leaving the stipulations, which constitute the essence of Israel's response, free of military obligations.
4 Lind, 'Paradigm', pp. 27-28, finds support in the basic agreement of the different Pentateuchal sources on the primacy of Yahweh's miracle at the sea.
5 *Op. cit.*, pp. 21-31.
6 *Yahweh is a Warrior*.

political power.[1] In the narratives which feature prophet-king cooperation Lind sees a more direct influence of the exodus tradition, for here the unaided efficacy of Yahweh's miracle has prominence.[2] Working forward from the exodus materials, Lind has offered a credible, if not conclusive, argument for how the exodus tradition may have influenced the Elisha cycle in a general way.[3] Significantly, several scholars working backward from the Elijah and Elisha stories have identified some rather clear-cut instances where these stories reflect exodus-related traditions in quite specific ways. Prominent here has been the identification of striking parallels linking Elijah with the figure of Moses.[4] In a recent discussion of this long-acknowledged parallelism Alan Jenks has provided the following helpful summary of 'the most obvious allusions to Mosaic traditions'.

> Elijah's receiving bread in the morning and meat in the evening (1 Kings 17.6, LXX; cf. Exodus 16.8, 12); his conflict with the Baal prophets (1 Kings 18.20-40), reminiscent of Moses' conflicts with the Egyptian magicians (Exodus 7.8-13, 20-22, etc.); Elijah's journey to Mount Horeb, where the Mosaic theophany seems to be recapitulated and reinterpreted (1 Kings 19; cf. Exodus 3; 19; 33–34); the passing of Elijah's authority to Elisha, reminding one of the Moses-Joshua relationship (1 Kings 19.16-21; 2 Kings 2; cf. Deuteronomy 31.14; 34.9); the manner of Elijah's death in an unknown place beyond the Jordan (2 Kings 2; cf. Deuteronomy 34.1-8).[5]

---

1 *Op. cit.*, pp. 132-38.
2 *Op. cit.*, pp. 138-44. Here Lind explicitly points to 2 Kgs 6.8-23 and 6.24–7.20 as prime examples of the exodus paradigm.
3 The following reviews are indicative of the generally favorable reception of Lind's overall thesis: Patrick D. Miller, in *BA* 44 (1981), pp. 188-89; Peter C. Craigie, in *Int* 36 (1982), p. 306; and James A. Rimbach, in *CBQ* 44 (1982), pp. 297-99.
4 See Fohrer, *Elia*, pp. 48-50; R.P. Carroll, 'The Elijah-Elisha Sagas: Some Remarks on Prophetic Succession in Ancient Israel', *VT* 19 (1969), pp. 400-15; and Frank M. Cross, *Canaanite Myth and Hebrew Epic* (Cambridge, MA: Harvard University Press, 1973), pp. 190-94.
5 Jenks, *The Elohist*, p. 95. See Cross, *Canaanite Myth*, pp. 190-94; Carroll, 'Elijah-Elisha Sagas', pp. 408-12, who points to more specific correspondences within some of these parallels.

3. The Stories in Contextual Perspective

The foregoing parallels do not appear to stop at the point of identifying Elijah as a 'new Moses'. The identity of Elisha is seen to be of concern here too. R.P. Carroll sees this in terms of a Deuteronomistic claim for a Mosaic prophetic succession, in which Elisha follows Elijah in fulfilling the promise of 'a prophet like Moses' (Deut. 18.15-18).[1] The oft-noted correspondences between the stories of Elijah and Elisha can be seen as reinforcing this view of Elisha's parallel identification with Moses.[2]

Certain factors would suggest that Elisha's connection to Moses might actually be secondary to his identification with the figure of Joshua. Elisha's parting of the Jordan river directly after the departure of his forerunner (2 Kgs 2) constitutes the most unmistakable link with Joshua (cf. Josh. 3–4).[3] To this could be added Elisha's immediately subsequent journey to Jericho, the city to which Joshua first advanced after crossing the Jordan (Josh. 5–6).[4] These links between Elisha and Joshua are reinforced by the parallel constitution of their respective names in terms of a reference to God attached to the verb יש*ע*, 'to save'.[5]

This last connection, associated as it is with military deliverance, might suggest a relationship between Elisha's role in Israel's warfare and that of Joshua. M.A. Beek has suggested precisely this relationship upon other, more specific grounds.[6] Beek argues that Elisha's epithet, 'the chariots and horsemen of Israel', derives from none other than the story of the exodus, which repeatedly juxtaposes the terms 'chariots and horse-

---

1 Carroll, 'Elijah-Elisha Sagas', pp. 401-403. Connecting the investiture of Elisha to Moses in terms of other emphases are R.A. Carlson, 'Élisée: Le Successeur d'Élie', *VT* 20 (1970), pp. 385-405; Ze'ev Weisman, 'The Personal Spirit as Imparting Authority', *ZAW* 93 (1981), pp. 225-34; Claude Coulot, 'L'investiture d'Élisée par Élie (1 R 19,19-21)', *RevScRel* 57 (1983), pp. 81-92.
2 See Carroll, 'Elijah-Elisha Sagas', pp. 411-13.
3 Jenks, *The Elohist*, p. 95.
4 *Ibid*.
5 The only scholar I know to have made explicit reference to this correspondence does so with a primary interest in pointing up the additional parallel to the name 'Jesus'. See Raymond E. Brown, 'Jesus and Elisha', *Perspective* 12 (1971), p. 101.
6 Beek, 'Meaning'.

men' to the point of making them a standardized symbol of foreign military power, as later contexts would tend to show.[1] Here he draws special attention to Joshua's destruction of the Canaanites' horses and chariots in Joshua 11. Prefaced as it is by the divine call to 'fear not', this episode is seen by Beek to be inherently related to the scene where Elisha tells his servant not to fear the surrounding host of Aramean horses and chariots (2 Kgs 6.16). The exodus tradition of the utter impotence and nullification of state-of-the-art weaponry is precisely what appears to be at the heart of each of these passages and the contexts within which they stand.

In the light of all of the foregoing connections, there is strong evidence that the exodus–conquest traditions played a distinct role in informing the war traditions of the Elisha cycle. While this situation is indicated by the continuities which we have noted, the full scope of the relationship between these two complexes would seem to include at least one important discontinuity as well. The Elisha cycle shows stark contrast with the exodus–conquest traditions in its ambivalent posture toward the destruction of the enemy.[2]

Israel's conflict with Aram as addressed in the Elisha cycle's final story (2 Kgs 13.14-20), projects the conventional intention to destroy the enemy completely but then presents a most unconventional explanation for why the preferred outcome will not take place, namely, because of the Israelite king's apparently unwitting failure to strike the ground more than three times with the arrows which are claimed, after the fact, to represent Israel's future blows against Aram. Israel's battle against the Moabites at the beginning of the cycle (2 Kgs 3) is strikingly similar in this regard. Reference is made to the killing of the enemy in accordance with traditional expectations (3.18, 24), but there follows a highly unusual justification for Israel's failure to carry out a complete destruction. Here

---

1 *Op. cit.*, pp. 5-7. Among the texts which Beek cites are Isa. 31.1, 3; 2 Kgs 18.21-24; Deut. 17.16.
2 The Elisha cycle's testimony to the destruction of the enemy would form the same basic contrast with the traditional paradigm of holy war as laid out by von Rad. Yet in light of the more solid and specific claims for the Elisha cycle's relationship with the exodus-conquest traditions, I have found better reason to treat this contrast only now.

3. The Stories in Contextual Perspective 141

the outcome is seen to rest solely and mysteriously upon the Moabite king's sacrifice of his firstborn son (3.27).

An even more subdued posture toward the destruction of the enemy becomes evident in the three Elisha stories which we have analyzed. Here the devastation of Aramean forces is either entirely by-passed in the divine objective by which Israel triumphs or else it is explicitly opposed by the prophet Elisha. In the story of the siege of Samaria (2 Kgs 6.24–7.20), Yahweh makes it possible for Israel to plunder the Arameans, but the Arameans are able to flee with 'their lives' (נפשם, 7.7). In the case of Naaman (2 Kgs 5), where the military nature of the conflict is admittedly less literal, it does not seem insignificant that even the plundering of the Aramean general by Gehazi is vigorously opposed by Elisha. The story which features the blinding of the Aramean army (2 Kgs 6.8-23) even goes to the point of highlighting a prophetic call for amnesty in the face of the king's eagerness to kill the captured Arameans. It is remarkable that Elisha insists on clemency for the Arameans here, especially in the light of the contemporary story of 1 Kings 20 which recounts prophetic judgment against another Israelite king who, after victorious battle againt the Arameans, fails to execute the ban (20.42).[1]

In light of the probable correspondences we have noted between the Elisha stories and the exodus–conquest traditions, all of these references to the survival of Israel's enemy seem to suggest a struggle to explain the variance of these outcomes from the more traditional pattern of divine salvation established in the exodus–conquest materials. In fact, the reference to Elisha's opposition to the king's call for executing the ban (2 Kgs 6.22) suggests nothing short of a direct challenge to the current relevance of the traditional pattern.[2] This view of the

---

1 Lind, *Yahweh is a Warrior*, p. 138, notes the contrast between these two stories in their relation to the ancient tradition of the ban. The contemporaneity of 1 Kings 20 with the Elisha cycle is strongly indicated by the reference to 'the sons of the prophets' (v. 35), as well as by the historical and canonical context given to the story. See Gray, *Kings*, p. 432.

2 The suggestion here that the Elisha materials were intended to exhibit contrast as well as correspondence with these earlier traditions is parallel to what has been seen in the Elijah story of 1 Kings 19. As Cross, *Canaanite Myth*, pp. 190-94, has argued, the theo-

matter comes into sharper focus as all of the lines of evidence which we have been pursuing are brought together.

Retracing our steps, we have seen that in the public life of ninth-century Israel no issue was more dominant than the Aramean military threat. The plentiful war references in the Elisha cycle not only reflected the threat itself, but also the centrality of the threat among the concerns of the prophetic circles of the time. Viewing these war references in the broader context of Israelite prophetic and warfare traditions shed light upon how the ninth-century prophets appear to have taken up this concern. We noted at least some evidence for seeing this prophetic focus upon the Aramean threat as the natural extension of a constitutive military role in early Israelite prophecy. In the absence of certainty for this possibility, however, we recognized some more substantial links between the prophets and the warfare of the ninth century. The identification of these prophets with older traditions of Yahweh's decisive involvement in Israel's warfare was plain to see. We saw definite indications here of a concern to revitalize these traditions in the face of a monarchical trend to abandon them. Yet our look at the striking evidences in the Elijah and Elisha stories for a conscious appropriation of the exodus–conquest traditions indicated that the prophetic concern for Israel's theology of warfare at this time may have involved even more. Over against clear continuities with the exodus tradition in affirming Yahweh as the deliverer of Israel, we noticed, specifically in the Elisha stories, a striking discontinuity with respect to the fate of the enemy, along with what seemed in each case to be a special concern to account for it.

This latter concern claims a rather likely place alongside the actual shape of the Aramean military threat. Just as the magnitude of this conflict would naturally have prompted Israel to pursue the relevance of its exodus theology of Yahweh's deliverance, so the grinding duration of this conflict would naturally have forced Israel to come to terms with the discrepancies in applying the exodus model to the current

phanic tradition of Moses is both paralleled and transcended in Yahweh's new revelatory encounter with Elijah. See Jenks, *The Elohist*, p. 97, who places this view alongside another option.

3. *The Stories in Contextual Perspective*   143

experience. As never before in its history, the Israelite nation found itself in a military situation where the classic pattern of Yahweh's deliverance would not have been easy to apply. Preserving the faith of Yahwism over against the sustained aggression and domination of Damascus would naturally have posed the need for finding fresh ways of perceiving how God might still be active in responding to Israel's need for deliverance.

The foregoing contextual considerations find a striking correlation with the content explicated earlier in our literary analysis of the three Elisha stories. Each of these stories is occupied from its opening statement onward with the problem of Aramean invasion. Even the story of Naaman, despite its lacking the explicit military thrust of the narrative of Benhadad's siege of Samaria, as introduced in 2 Kgs 6.24, and Aram's repeated ambushes on Israel, as introduced in 2 Kgs 6.8, is set in reference to the military issue by the preliminary attention given to Naaman's identity as an Aramean general who has been victorious over Israel (2 Kgs 5.1). The military overtones of Naaman's intrusion into Israelite territory are never far below the surface, as can be seen in the Israelite king's initial reaction, 'see how he is seeking a fight with me!' (v. 7), and in Elisha's final word, which links Gehazi's acquisitions to military plunder (v. 26).

Even as the Aramean threat sets the stage for each of these stories, the countering of Aramean designs is crucial to the goal of each story. Benhadad's siege of Samaria is dramatically broken (2 Kgs 7.7), Aramean raids on Israelite territory are abruptly ended (2 Kgs 6.23), and Naaman's intent to put the king and prophet of Israel in his service is completely turned around (2 Kgs 5.15). And the ultimate source and theological claim behind these outcomes is in full accord with our contextual considerations—salvation is from the Lord.[1] We saw earlier how the stories in each case pushed past the affirmation of Elisha's saving role to bear witness to Yahweh's supremacy in salvation. Thus, Naaman is led beyond the discovery 'that there is a prophet in Israel' (2 Kgs 5.8) to the con-

---

1   So Ps. 3.8. See also Hos. 13.4, where virtually the same affirmation is explictly tied to the exodus event.

144 *God Saves*

fession 'that there is no God in all the earth but in Israel' (v. 15). Similarly, when the Arameans realize that their ambush plans are being perceived somehow by the prophet Elisha, who is initially identified for us simply as 'the man of God' (2 Kgs 6.9), they set their sights on Elisha, only to discover through Elisha's prayers that Yahweh controls all sight in the interest of his own salvific designs. The saving power of Yahweh is highlighted just as clearly when the sudden deliverance of Samaria from Benhadad's siege unfolds outside the city as an unexpected fulfillment of the entrapped prophet's 'word of the Lord' (2 Kgs 7.1, 16).

Further correspondence with the proposed background can be found in the way we saw each of these stories depicting Israelite resistance to Yahweh's coming salvation. The portrayal of such resistance among Israelite royalty is especially pertinent to our case for monarchical departure from Yahwistic warfare traditions. We saw how the anxious reaction of Israel's king to Naaman's appearance is marked by its complete impotence in pointing the general toward his healing and its divine source (2 Kgs 5.7-8). In the siege of Samaria the Israelite court's obstruction of God's salvation manifests itself at several points—when the king attacks Elisha after his own fasting has not availed (2 Kgs 6.30-31), when the king's captain registers mocking skepticism toward Elisha's prediction of deliverance (7.2), and when the king resists sending starving horses to see whether reports of the city's deliverance might be true (7.12).

We saw, however, that the given stories are not sociologically fixated in identifying opposition toward divine salvation. Thus, Elisha's servant, Gehazi, acts in diametric opposition to the divine direction of Naaman's deliverance, as perceived by Elisha (2 Kgs 5.26-27). The cannibalism of the commoners within Samaria likewise stands forth in counterpoint to the process of divine deliverance when it is seen in its proper contrast to the mutual support of the starving lepers outside the city (2 Kgs 6.28-29; 7.3, 9). To a lesser extent, even the panic of Elisha's servant at the ambush of Dothan can be seen to represent Israelite resistance to the salvation which Yahweh is bringing (2 Kgs 6.15).[1]

Our proposed background suggested that in addition to the theological struggle over *whether* Yahweh is saving Israel, the ninth-century prophets had to face the issue of *how* Yahweh is saving Israel. For if monarchical trends were encouraging Israelites, especially royal ones, to dismiss the validity of Yahwistic warfare, the continuing survival and success of Aram were undoubtedly prompting Israelites, even conservative ones, to question the full applicability of this tradition. Here again the literary content we saw in the three stories corresponds strikingly to the suggested context. Beyond the shared tradition that salvation comes from Yahweh, we saw that the central thrust of each story is to teach something distinctive and new about how this salvation comes about, and this is reinforced in each case by Elisha's special efforts to get unwitting and distracted Israelites to see it. Thus, in the Naaman story, the test of 'standing before the Lord' is lifted up as the way through which Yahweh's deliverance can come to an Aramean general and depart from an Israelite servant.[2] These outcomes serve to reinterpret this time of Aramean domination as a time when Yahweh's salvation is nonetheless manifest, albeit in unconventional and unexpected ways. Thus, as Elisha informs Gehazi at the end of the story, it is not a time when Israelites should expect to plunder the Arameans (5.26), but, in keeping with the narrator's comment at the beginning of the story, it is a time when an Aramean general must submit to Yahweh as the sole source of even Aramean salvation (5.1).[3]

---

1 One could compare Elisha's 'Fear not!' here to Jesus' sharp statement to his disciples before calming the sea, 'You of little faith, why are you so afraid?' (Matt. 8.26). In both of these stories the fear of the moment, which would normally be appropriate, is measured against a context in which multiple deliverances have just been performed through the leader's agency.
2 We saw this message reinforced by the role played by servants in directing Naaman to his healing and by the motif of servanthood, which occurs at every turn, to include Naaman's moment of truth and confirming encounter with Elisha.
3 Note the use of the noun תשועה, salvation, in the statement, 'Yahweh had given *victory* to Aram'.

The story of the blinding of the Aramean army, as seen in our literary study, also speaks freshly and distinctively to the problem of perceiving the present shape of Yahweh's salvation. The key insight here is that Yahweh preserves (שמר) Israel. However, the subtlety of this divine operation, as we noted, leaves it easily overlooked not only by Aramean presumption but also by Israelite anxiety. Responding to Elisha's prayers, Yahweh opens Israelite eyes and blinds Aramean eyes in order that both can see what earlier had gone unrecognized. However, this purpose for Yahweh's intervention is not immediately apparent, for rather than seeing a revelation of Yahweh's earlier action to preserve (שמר), the Israelite king sees only a present chance to strike (נכה). Only when the Arameans themselves are shown salvation in Samaria (שמרון) is everyone able to see the preserving power and will of Yahweh who oversees the ever-open course of history.

Of these three narratives, the story of the siege of Samaria is the most explicit in addressing the issue of how Yahweh saves Israel. The question is clearly posed at the heart of the story by the king's captain in response to Elisha's oracle of salvation, 'If Yahweh made windows in heaven, could this thing be?' (7.2). These words skeptically raise the question of divine means, and the rest of the story answers this question in surprising fashion. Yahweh's salvation comes not from above, as the captain's question teases, but rather from the unwitting agency of four outcast lepers. Yet we saw another, more decisive, contrast involved here. The mutual support of the lepers outside the city is presented in stark contrast to the destructive contention among the people inside. Detecting no help from Yahweh, the insiders excuse themselves from helping one another, as we saw in the king's response to the woman's cry for help (ישע), 'If Yahweh will not help you, how can I help you?' (6.27). The lepers, on the other side, by becoming sources of help to one another, become agents of salvation for Yahweh. Whereas the king's garment-rending question assumes a tradition-attested dichotomy between his help and God's, the story ingeniously shows how human help and Yahweh's salvation are now being woven together in new and marvelous ways.

3. The Stories in Contextual Perspective 147

In conclusion, I have shown in this chapter that, whereas the contextual matrices which have been proposed or implied in past interpretations of the given Elisha stories show varying degrees of incompatibility with the content explicated in our literary-aesthetic analysis, there is a thoroughgoing correlation between this content and the context of theological struggle with Aramean domination, which I have here delineated. It is my argument that the foregoing demonstration of this harmony of content and context properly locates the governing typicality[1] of these stories in the attempt to offer fresh insight into Yahweh's saving activity in ninth-century Israel. On this basis, I see justification for designating these stories as *didactic salvation stories*. As such, these stories, each in their own way, as we have seen, freshly expound the deeply rooted theological message of Elisha's own name, 'God saves'.[2]

---

1 For this term, see Knierim, 'Form Criticism Reconsidered', p. 456.
2 It has been common for scholars to link the mission and stories of Elijah with the meaning of his name 'Yahweh is God', e.g. Martin Noth, *Die israelitischen Personennamen in Rahmen der gemeinsemitischen Namengebung* (BWANT, III/10; Stuttgart: W. Kohlhammer, 1928), pp. 140-41; Gray, *Kings*, pp. 358-59; Bronner, *Stories of Elijah and Elisha*, pp. 22-23; Rudolf Smend, 'Der biblische und der historische Elia', *VTS* 28 (1975), p. 177; Jones, *Kings*, p. 303; DeVries, *1 Kings*, p. 216. But I have found no one who makes any such direct connection between the name and the stories of Elisha. Ellul, *Politics of God*, pp. 10-11, comes close to this connection when he acknowledges the same meaning for the names of Elisha and Jesus.

Chapter 4

CONCLUSION

The preceding chapters have called for and offered a fresh interpretation of the three main Elisha stories of 2 Kings 5–7. It is my purpose in this concluding chapter to present a brief summary of my results and comment on their implications for biblical studies.

My review of past scholarship has shown how efforts to classify the Elisha stories have dominated interpretation of these narratives since Gunkel. For most of this century scholarship has unanimously followed Gunkel's lead in identifying these narratives with the purpose of venerating the prophet Elisha. Closer investigations into the context and the content of these narratives have led several scholars more recently to propose larger, more substantial purposes for the stories. Accordingly, these narratives have been viewed as polemics against Baal worship,[1] as didactic material aimed at transforming the simple legend,[2] as apologetics for the prophetic office,[3] or as social satire against the ruling establishment.[4]

I have demonstrated how these diverse proposals are flawed in varying degrees by the tendency to stress certain aspects of the content and context of these narratives to the neglect of others. Against those who would call for more open-ended literary explorations which relinquish the prospect of identifying these stories in terms of a specific typicality of function and

---

1 Bronner, *Stories of Elijah and Elisha*.
2 Rofé, 'Classes', pp. 145-53.
3 Long, 'Social Setting', pp. 46-58. See DeVries, *Prophet against Prophet*, pp. 52-92.
4 LaBarbera, 'Man of War'. See Brueggemann, *2 Kings*, pp. 1-6; Gottwald, *Hebrew Bible*, pp. 351-52.

meaning,[1] I have shown how a thorough investigation of literary features and contextual factors calls for understanding these three narratives as didactic salvation stories set against the Aramean military threat of ninth-century Israel. Thus, in addition to an ingenious literary artistry, these stories exhibit a profound and timely theological message which has long been overlooked in biblical scholarship.[2]

With respect to the broader scope of biblical studies, this study yields certain methodological, historical and theological

---

1 Hobbs, *2 Kings*, pp. 17, 45; Long, *1 Kings*, pp. 181-94.
2 My own study corroborates and extends the rich insight of the studies of Cohn (on 2 Kgs 5) and LaBarbera (on 6.8–7.20) on the literary integrity and ingenuity of each of the three stories, but I have gone well beyond them in showing the full scope and thrust of the literary design in relation to Yahwism's theological struggle with Aramean domination. Even Brueggemann, who has appreciated the theological dimension of these stories like no other biblical scholar to date (see *2 Kings*, but also his most recent study of 6.8-23, 'Embarrassing Footnote'), has tended to restrict the import of the text's theological claims to the class conflict which LaBarbera stresses. Consequently, while Brueggemann is able to see the text's concern for whether Yahweh saves over against prevailing royal notions, he is less able to see the text's concern for how Yahweh saves over against Yahwism's own earlier traditions. Interestingly, Ellul, *Politics of God*, who writes from outside the ranks of biblical scholars, has come closest to recognizing the text's theological intent to show how Yahweh saves (see pp. 10-12, 21-22), although Ellul has self-consciously not concerned himself with how this fits into 'the spiritual history' of Israel nor why it was written at this period in political history' (p. 12 n. 2). This last point, along with the fact that Ellul's exposition does not offer a comprehensive treatment of the given narratives (6.8-23 is not treated at all) with biblical-critical awareness, has probably caused his analysis to be taken as offering more a reflection upon the text than a reflection of the text. I see my own study as having vindicated Ellul's basic insight into the theological thrust of certain Elisha stories, offering a literary scope and specificity, a contextual identity and clarity, and a critical grounding, which Ellul's study does not offer or attempt. However, with respect to methodology, I wonder as I come to the end of this study whether it is less Ellul's approach than the one I represent which needs to be vindicated. I am struck by Ellul's introductory disclaimer concerning his posture toward historical critical methods: 'In our view these inner researches, though they are of value, are definitely restricted in scope, and only very relatively offer a deeper exposition of the text of the Bible. We shall adopt the simple attitude of the believer with his Bible who through the text that he reads is ultimately trying to discover what is the Word of God, and what is the final meaning of his life in the presence of this text' (p. 12 n. 2).

4. Conclusion

implications. While I have not presumed to offer any definitive method for narrative classification, my own treatment of the Elisha stories, as well as my critique of past research, offers general support to the view that integration, not dichotomization, of literary and historical approaches represents the way forward in biblical interpretation.[1]

Historically, my work points toward higher levels of literary sophistication and theological deliberation among pre-classical prophetic circles than have typically been acknowledged.[2] Accordingly, my results may prove to be important for opening up fresh light on the antecedents of eighth-century prophecy.[3]

Finally, the theological dimension of my thesis may have some indirect relevance for at least one query in New Testament studies. On the basis of similarities between the Elisha stories and the Gospels with respect to the types and descriptions of their recorded miracles, Raymond E. Brown has argued that the Elisha cycle suggests 'a more satisfactory analogue for the pre-Gospel miracle collections' than any yet proposed.[4] My study offers a basis for strengthening and extending this argument, for the miracle accounts of Elisha

---

1 See the valuable collection of articles in *The Poet and the Historian: Essays in Literary and Historical Biblical Criticism* (ed. Richard Elliot Friedman; HSM, 26; Chico, CA: Scholars, 1963). An especially penetrating and compelling case for the inseparability of historical and literary approaches to Scripture has recently been offered by Stephen A. Geller, 'Through Windows and Mirrors into the Bible: History, Literature, and Language in the Study of the Text', in *A Sense of the Text: The Art of Language in the Study of Biblical Literature* (Jewish Quarterly Review Supplement; Winona Lake, IN: Eisenbrauns, 1983), pp. 3-40.
2 The fresh and sweeping proposal offered recently by Anthony F. Campbell, *Of Prophets and Kings: A Late Ninth-Century Document (1 Samuel 1–2 Kings 10)* (CBQ Monograph Series, 17; Washington, DC: Catholic Biblical Association of America, 1986), moves in a similar direction by attributing all of 1 Sam. 1–2 Kgs 10 to the literary activity and theological agenda of the disciples of Elisha.
3 See Menahem Haran, 'From Early to Classical Prophecy: Continuity and Change', *VT* 27 (1977), pp. 385-97, for a representative view of the more limited perceptions which have heretofore been accepted.
4 Brown, 'Jesus and Elisha', pp. 98-99. Cf. D. Gerald Bostock, 'Jesus as the New Elisha', *ExpTim* 92 (1980), pp. 39-41; and Thomas Louis Brodie, 'Jesus as the New Elisha: Cracking the Code', *ExpTim* 93 (1981), pp. 39-42.

treated here, like the miracle accounts of Jesus in the Gospels, have been shown to be profoundly occupied with revealing God's new and surprising work of salvation. Thus, even in terms of the broader theological agenda of the Gospel narratives, the stories of Elisha may represent an extremely important antecedent.[1]

---

[1] Such a possibility would appear to be relevant to the recent efforts of Wolfgang M.W. Roth, 'The Secret of the Kingdom', *The Christian Century* 100 (1983), pp. 179-82; and *Hebrew Gospel: Cracking the Code of Mark* (Oak Park, IL: Meyer Stone Books, 1988), who sees the Elisha cycle in its larger arrangement as pointing toward the operative model behind the form of the Gospel of Mark.

BIBLIOGRAPHY

Ackerman, James S. 'Prophecy and Warfare in Early Israel: A Study of the Deborah-Barak Story'. *BASOR* 220 (1975): 5-15.
Albright, William F. 'A Votive Stele Erected by Ben-Hadad of Damascus to the God of Melcarth'. *BASOR* 87 (1942): 23-29.
Alter, Robert. *The Art of Biblical Narrative*. New York: Basic Books, 1981.
Anderson, George W. 'Israel: Amphictyony: 'AM; KĀHĀL; 'ĒDÂH'. In *Translating and Understanding the Old Testament: Essays in Honor of Herbert G. May*, pp. 135-51. Ed. H.T. Frank and W.L. Reed. Nashville: Abingdon Press, 1970.
Bach, Robert. *Die Aufforderungen zur Flucht und zum Kampf im alttestamentlichen Prophetenspruch*. WMANT, 9. Neukirchen: Neukirchener Verlag, 1962.
Bardtke, Hans. 'Naeman'. In *Biblisch-historisches Handwörterbuch*, vol. 2, col. 1279. Ed. Leonhard Rost and Bo Reicke. Göttingen: Vandenhoeck & Ruprecht, 1964.
Barnes, William E. *The Second Book of Kings*, Cambridge: Cambridge University Press, 1928.
Barrick, W. Boyd. 'Elisha and the Magic Bow: A Note on 2 Kings xiii 15-17'. *VT* 35 (1985): 355-63.
Beek, M.A. 'The Meaning of the Expression "The Chariots and the Horsemen of Israel" (II Kings ii 12)'. *OTS* 17 (1972): 1-10.
Begg, Christopher T. '2 Kings 20.12-19 as an Element of the Deuteronomistic History'. *CBQ* 48 (1986): 27-38.
Bentzen, Aage. *Introduction to the Old Testament*. 2 vols. 6th edn Copenhagen: G.E.C. Gad, 1961.
Berlin, Adele. *Poetics and Interpretation of Biblical Narrative*. Bible and Literature Series. Sheffield: Almond Press, 1983.
Blank, Sheldon. *Understanding the Prophets*. New York: Union of American Hebrew Congregations, 1969.
Blenkinsopp, Joseph. *A History of Prophecy in Israel: From the Settlement in the Land to the Hellenistic Period*. Philadelphia: Westminster, 1983.
Bostock, D. Gerald. 'Jesus as the New Elisha'. *ExpTim* 92 (1980): 39-41.
Bright, John. *A History of Israel*. 3rd edn. Philadelphia: Westminster, 1981.
Brodie, Thomas Louis. 'Jesus as the New?? Elisha: Cracking the Code'. *ExpTim* 93 (1981): 39-42.
Bronner, Leah. *The Stories of Elijah and Elisha as Polemics against Baal Worship*. Leiden: Brill, 1968.
Brown, Francis, Driver, S.R., Briggs, C.A., eds. *A Hebrew and English Lexicon of the Old Testament*. Oxford: Clarendon Press, 1907.

Brown, Raymond E. 'Jesus and Elisha'. *Perspective* 12 (1971): 85-104.
Brueggemann, Walter. 'The Embarrassing Footnote'. *Theology Today* 44 (1987): 5-14.
—*2 Kings*. Knox Preaching Guides. Atlanta: John Knox Press, 1982.
Buber, Martin. *Königtum Gottes*. 3rd edn. Heidelberg: L. Schneider, 1956.
Burney, Charles F. *Notes on the Hebrew Text of the Book of Kings*. Oxford: Clarendon, 1903.
Buss, Martin J. 'The Study of Forms'. In *Old Testament Form Criticism*, pp. 1-56. Ed. John H. Hayes. San Antonio: Trinity University Press, 1979.
Campbell, Anthony F. *Of Prophets and Kings: A Late Ninth-Century Document (1 Samuel 1–2 Kings 10)*. CBQ Monograph Series, 17. Washington, DC: Catholic Biblical Association of America, 1986.
Carlson, R.A. 'Élisée: Le Successeur d'Élie'. *VT* 20 (1979): 385-405.
Carroll, Robert P. 'The Elijah-Elisha Sagas: Some Remarks on Prophetic Succession in Ancient Israel'. *VT* 19 (1969): 400-15.
—*When Prophecy Failed: Cognitive Dissonance in the Prophetic Traditions of the Old Testament*. New York: Seabury, 1979.
Childs, Brevard S. *Introduction to the Old Testament as Scripture*. Philadelphia: Fortress, 1979.
—'On Reading the Elijah Narratives'. *Int* 34 (1980): 128-37.
—'A Traditio-Historical Study of the Reed Sea Tradition'. *VT* 20 (1979): 406-18.
Coats, George W. 'Genres: Why Should They Be Important for Exegesis?' In *Saga, Legend, Tale, Novella, Fable. Narrative Forms in Old Testament Literature*, pp. 7-15. Ed. George W. Coats. JSOTS, 35. Sheffield: JSOT, 1985.
Cohn, Robert L. 'Form and Perspective in 2 Kings V'. *VT* 31 (1983): 171-84.
Coulot, Claude. 'L'investiture d'Élisée par Élie (1 R 19,19-21)'. *RevScRel* 57 (1983): 81-92.
Craigie, Peter C. *The Problem of War in the Old Testament*. Grand Rapids: Eerdmans, 1978.
—Review of *Yahweh is a Warrior* by Millard C. Lind. *Int* 36 (1982): 306.
Crenshaw, James L. *Gerhard von Rad*. Makers of the Modern Theological Mind. Waco, TX: Word Books, 1978.
—*Old Testament Wisdom: An Introduction*. Atlanta: John Knox, 1981.
—'Prolegomenon'. In *Studies in Ancient Israelite Wisdom*. Ed. J.L. Crenshaw. New York: KTAV, 1976.
—*Prophetic Conflict: Its Effect upon Israelite Religion*. BZAW, 124. Berlin: de Gruyter, 1971.
—Review of *Wisdom in Israel*, by Gerhard von Rad. *RSR* 2 (1976): 6-12.
—*Samson: A Secret Betrayed, A Vow Ignored*. Atlanta: John Knox, 1978.
Cross, Frank M. 'The Song of the Sea and Canaanite Myth'. *JTC* 5 (1968): 1-25.
—'The Themes of the Book of Kings and the Structure of the Deuteronomistic History'. In *Canaanite Myth and Hebrew Epic*, pp. 274-89. Cambridge, MA: Harvard University Press, 1973.

Cross, Frank M. and Freedman, David N. 'The Song of Miriam'. *JNES* 14 (1955): 237-50.
Culley, Robert C. 'Punishment Stories in the Legends of the Prophets'. In *Orientation by Disorientation: Studies in Literary Criticism and Biblical Literary Criticism*, pp. 167-81. Ed. Richard A. Spencer. Pittsburgh: Pickwick, 1980.
—'Structural Analysis: Is it Done with Mirrors?' *Int* 28 (1974): 165-81.
—'Themes and Variations in Three Groups of OT Narratives'. *Semeia* 3 (1975): 3-13.
DeVries, Simon J. *I Kings*. Word Biblical Commentary, vol. 12. Waco, TX: Word Books, 1985.
—*Prophet against Prophet: The Role of the Micaiah Narrative (I Kings 22) in the Development of Early Prophetic Tradition*. Grand Rapids: Eerdmans, 1978.
—'Temporal Terms as Structural Elements in the Holy War Tradition'. *VT* 25 (1975): 80-105.
—*Yesterday, Today and Tomorrow*. Grand Rapids: Eerdmans, 1975.
Dietrich, Walter. *Prophetie und Geschichte. Eine redaktionsgeschichtliche Untersuchung zum deuteronomistischen Geschichtswerk*. FRLANT, 108. Göttingen: Vandenhoeck & Ruprecht, 1972.
Dommershausen, W. *Die Esterrolle. Stil und Ziel einer alttestamentlichen Schrift*. Stuttgart: Katholisches Bibelwerk, 1968.
Donner, Herbert. 'The Separate States of Israel and Judah'. In *Israelite and Judaean History*, pp. 381-434. Ed. John H. Hayes and J. Maxwell Miller. Philadelphia: Westminster, 1977.
Eissfeldt, Otto. *Einleitung in das Alte Testament*. Tübingen: Mohr, 1934.
—'Das zweite Buch der Könige'. In *Die Heilige Schrift des Alten Testaments*, vol. 1, pp. 540-600. Ed. A. Bertholet. Tübingen: Mohr, 1935.
Ellis, Peter F. '1-2 Kings'. In *Jerome Biblical Commentary*, vol. 1, pp. 179-209. Ed. Raymond E. Brown, Joseph Fitzmyer, and Roland E. Murphy. Englewood Cliffs: Prentice Hall, 1968.
Ellul, Jacques. *The Politics of God and the Politics of Man*. Trans. Geoffrey W. Bromiley. Grand Rapids: Eerdmans, 1972.
Fannon, P. '1 and 2 Kings'. *A New Catholic Commentary of Holy Scripture*, pp. 328-51. Ed. Reginald C. Fuller and Leonard Johnson. London: Thomas Nelson and Sons, 1969.
Fohrer, Georg. 'Altes Testament: "Amphiktyonie" und "Bund"'. *TLZ* 111 (1966): 801-16.
—*Einleitung in das Alte Testament*. Heidelberg: Quelle & Meyer, 1965.
—*Elia*. 2nd edn. ATANT, 53. Zürich: Zwingli, 1968.
—*Geschichte der israelitischen Religion*. Berlin: de Gruyter, 1969.
Fretheim, Terence E. *Deuteronomic History*. Nashville: Abingdon, 1983.
Friedman, Richard Elliot, ed. *The Poet and the Historian: Essays in Literary and Historical Biblical Criticism*. HSM, 26. Chico, CA: Scholars, 1983.
Galling, Kurt. 'Der Ehrenname Elisas und die Entrückung Elias'. *ZTK* 53 (1956): 131-35.
Geller, Stephen A. 'Through Windows and Mirrors into the Bible. History, Literature, and Language in the Study of the Text'. In *A Sense of the*

Text: *The Art of Language in the Study of Biblical Literature*, pp. 3-40. Jewish Quarterly Review Supplement. Winona Lake, IN: Eisenbrauns, 1983.
Gibson, J.C.L. and Driver, G.R. *Canaanite Myths and Legends*. Rev. edn. Edinburgh: T. & T. Clark, 1977.
Gilbert, Pierre. 'Légende ou Saga?' *VT* 24 (1974): 411-20.
Good, Edwin M. Review of *Literary Criticism of the Old Testament*, by Norman Habel. *JBL* 92 (1973): 287-89.
Gordon, Cyrus H. *Ugaritic Textbook*. Analecta Orientalia, 38. 2nd edn. with suppl. Rome: Pontificium Institutum Biblicum, 1967.
Gottwald, Norman K. 'War, Holy'. *IDBSup*, pp. 942-44. Ed. Keith Crim. Nashville: Abingdon, 1962.
—*All the Kingdoms of the Earth: Israelite Prophecy and International Relations in the Ancient Near East*. New York: Harper & Row, 1964.
—*The Tribes of Yahweh: A Sociology of the Religion of Liberated Israel 1250-1050 BCE*. Maryknoll, NY: Orbis, 1979.
—*The Hebrew Bible: A Socio-Literary Introduction*. Philadelphia: Fortress Press, 1985.
—ed. *Social Scientific Criticism of the Hebrew Bible: The Israelite Monarchy*. Semeia, 37. Decatur, GA: Scholars, 1986.
Gray, John. *I & II Kings: A Commentary*. 2nd edn. Philadelphia: Westminster, 1963.
Greenstein, Edward L. 'Biblical Narratology'. *Prooftexts* 1 (1981): 201-208.
Greimas, A.J. *Semantique structurale*. Paris: Larousse, 1966.
—*Du sens: Essais sémiotiques*. Paris: Seuil, 1970.
Gressmann, Hugo. 'Sage und Geschichte in den Patriarchenerzählungen'. *ZAW* 30 (1910): 1-34.
—*Mose und seine Zeit: Ein Kommentar zu den Mose-Sagen*. FRLANT, 18. Göttingen: Vandenhoeck & Ruprecht, 1913.
—*Die älteste Geschichtsschreibung und Prophetie Israels*. SAT, 2/1. 2nd edn. Göttingen: Vandenhoeck & Ruprecht, 1921.
Gros Louis, Kenneth R.R. 'Elijah and Elisha'. In *Literary Interpretations of Biblical Narratives*, pp. 177-90. Ed. K.R.R. Gros Louis. Nashville: Abingdon, 1974.
Gunkel, Hermann. *Genesis*. HKAT, I.1. Göttingen: Vandenhoeck & Ruprecht, 1901.
—*The Legends of Genesis*. Trans. W.H. Carruth. Chicago: Open Court, 1901; reprint edn with an introduction by William F. Albright. New York: Schocken, 1964.
—'Die Grundprobleme der israelitischen Literaturgeschichte'. *DLZ* 27 (1906): 1797-1800, 186.
—'Die israelitische Literatur'. In *Die orientalischen Literaturen*, pp. 53-112. Ed. P. Hinneberg. KdG, 1/7. Leipzig: Teubner, 1906.
—*Elias, Jahve und Baal*. Religionsgeschichtliche Volksbücher, 2/2, pp. 1-76. Tübingen: Mohr, 1906.
—*Geschichten von Elisa*. Meisterwerke hebräischer Erzählungskunst, 1. Berlin: Karl Curtius, 1925.

—'Fundamental Problems of Hebrew Literary History'. In *What Remains of the Old Testament? And Other Essays*, pp. 57-58. Trans. A.K. Dallas. New York: Macmillan, 1928.

—'Elisha—The Successor of Elijah (2 Kings ii.1-18)'. *ExpTim* 41 (1929-1930): 182-86.

—'Sagen und Legenden: II'. In *RGG*, 2nd edn, vol. 5, cols. 49-60. Ed. H. Gunkel and L. Zscharnack. Tübingen: J.C.B. Mohr, 1931.

—*Die israelitische Literatur*. Darmstadt: Wissenschaftliche Buchgesellschaft, 1963.

Hahn, Herbert F. *The Old Testament in Modern Research*. Philadelphia: Fortress, 1966.

Hals, Ronald M. 'Legend: A Case Study in Old Testament Form Critical Terminology'. *CBQ* 34 (1972): 166-76.

Haran, Menahem. 'From Early to Classical Prophecy; Continuity and Change'. *VT* 27 (1977): 385-97.

Harrison, R.K. 'Healing'. *IDB* vol. 2, pp. 541-46. Ed. George A. Buttrick. Nashville: Abingdon, 1962.

—'Leprosy'. *IDB*. vol. 3, pp. 111-13. Ed. George A. Buttrick. Nashville: Abingdon, 1962.

Heller, Jan. 'Drei Wundertaten Elisas'. *Communio Viatorum* 2 (1959): 83-85.

Hentschel, Georg. 'Die Heilung Naamans'. In *Künder des Wortes*, pp. 11-21. Ed. L. Ruppert, P. Weimar and E. Zenger. Würzburg: Echter, 1982.

Hermann, Siegfried. *A History of Israel in Old Testament Times*. Trans. John Bowden. Philadelphia; Fortress, 1975.

Hobbs, T.R. '2 Kings 1 and 2: Their Unity and Purpose'. *SR* 13 (1984): 327-34.

—*2 Kings*. Word Biblical Commetary 13. Waco, TX: Word Books, 1985.

Hossfeld, F.L. and Meyer, I. *Prophet gegen Prophet: Eine Analyse der alttestamentlichen Texte zum Thema: Wahre und falsche Propheten*. Biblische Beiträge 9. Fribourg: Schweizerisches Katholisches Bibelwerk, 1973.

Houtman, Cornelis. 'Elia's hemelvaart: notities over en naar aanleiding van 2 Koningen 2.1-18'. *NedTTs* 32 (1978): 283-304.

Hylmö, Gunnar. *Gamla Testamentets Litteraturhistoria*. Lund: Gleerup, 1938.

Jackson, Jared J., Kessler, Martin, eds. *Rhetorical Criticism: Essays in Honor of James Muilenburg*. Pittsburgh: Pickwick, 1974.

Jenks, Alan W. *The Elohist and North Israelite Traditions*. SBLMS 22. Missoula: Scholars, 1977.

Jepsen, Alfred. 'Israel und Damaskus'. *AFO* 14 (1942): 154-58.

—*Die Quellen des Königsbuches*. Halle: Max Niemeyer, 1953.

Jolles, André. *Einfache Formen*. Darmstadt: Wissenschaftliche Buchgesellschaft, 1930.

Jones, Gwilym H. '"Holy War" or "Yahweh War"?' *VT* 25 (1975): 642-58.

—*1 and 2 Kings*. 2 vols. New Century Bible Commentary. Grand Rapids: Eerdmans, 1984.

Kaiser, Otto. *Introduction to the Old Testament*. Trans. John Sturdy. Minneapolis: Augsburg, 1977.

Kaufmann, Yehezkel. *The Religion of Israel, From its Beginnings to the Babylonian Exile*. Trans. Moshe Greenberg. New York: Schocken, 1972.
Keller, C.A. 'Die Gefährdung der Ahnfrau. Ein Beitrag zur gattungs- und motivgeschichtlichen Erforschung alttestamentlicher Erzählungen'. *ZAW* 61 (1954): 181.
Kessler, Martin. 'A Methodological Setting for Rhetorical Criticism'. In *Art and Meaning: Rhetoric in Biblical Literature*, pp. 1-19. Ed. David J.A. Clines, David M. Gunn, and Alan J. Hauser. JSOT Supplement Series 19. Sheffield: JSOT, 1982.
Knierim, Rolf. 'Old Testament Form Criticism Reconsidered' *Int* 27 (1973): 435-68.
—'Criticism of Literary Features, Form, Tradition and Redaction'. In *The Hebrew Bible and its Modern Interpreters*, pp. 123-65. Ed. Douglas A. Knight and Gene M. Tucker. Philadelphia: Fortress, 1985. Chico, CA: Scholars, 1985.
Knight, Douglas A. 'The Understanding of *'Sitz im Leben'* in Form Criticism'. In *Society of Biblical Literature Seminar Papers 1974*. vol. 1, pp. 105-25. Missoula: Scholars, 1974.
Koch, Klaus. *The Growth of the Biblical Tradition: The Form Critical Method*. Trans. S.M. Cupitt. New York: Charles Scribner's Sons, 1969.
Kuenen, Abraham. *Historisch-kritische Einleitung in die Bücher des Alten Testaments*. vol. 1, pt. 2. Trans. Th. Weber. Leipzig: Schulze, 1885.
LaBarbera, Robert. 'The Man of War and The Man of God: Social Satire in 2 Kings 6.8–7.20'. *CBQ* 46 (1984): 637-51.
Licht, Jacob. 'Story Telling in the Bible'. *Immanuel* 7 (1977): 21-24.
—*Storytelling in the Bible*. Jerusalem: Magnes, 1978.
Lind, Millard C. 'Paradigm of Holy War in the Old Testament'. *BR* 16 (1971): 16-31.
—*Yahweh is a Warrior: The Theology of Warfare in Ancient Israel*. Scottdale, PA: Herald, 1980.
Lindars, Barnabas. 'Elijah, Elisha and the Gospel Miracles'. In *Miracles*, pp. 63-79. Ed. C.F.D. Moule. London: Mowbray, 1965.
Long, Burke O. 'II Kings 3: An Oracular Fulfillment Narrative'. In *Society of Biblical Literature Seminar Papers 1971*, vol. 1, pp. 183-205. Missoula: Scholars, 1971.
—'The Effect of Divination upon Israelite Literature'. *JBL* 92 (1973): 489-97.
—'2 Kings III and Genres of Prophetic Narrative'. *VT* 23 (1973): 337-48.
—'The Social Setting for Prophetic Miracle Stories'. *Semeia* 3 (1975): 46-63.
—'Recent Field Studies in Oral Literature and the Question of *Sitz im Leben*'. *Semeia* 5 (1976): 33-49.
—'Recent Field Studies in Oral Literature and Their Bearing on OT Criticism'. *VT* 26 (1976): 187-98.
—'Prophetic Authority as Social Reality'. In *Canon and Authority: Essays in Old Testament Religion and Theology*, pp. 3-20. Ed. George W. Coats and Burke O. Long. Philadelphia: Fortress, 1977.
—'Some Recent Trends in the Form Criticism of Old Testament Narratives'. *Proceedings of the Seventh World Congress of Jewish Studies: Studies*

in the Bible and the Ancient Near East. Jerusalem: World Union of Jewish Studies, 1981.

—'Artistry in Hebrew Historical Narrative: Observations on 1–2 Kings'. *Proceedings of the Eight World Congress of Jewish Studies: The Period of the Bible*. Jerusalem: World Union of Jewish Studies, 1982.

—'The Social World of Ancient Israel'. *Int* 37 (1982): 243-55.

—*I Kings with An Introduction to Historical Literature*. Forms of Old Testament Literature 9. Grand Rapids: Eerdmans, 1984.

—'Historical Narrative and the Fictionalizing Imagination'. *VT* 35 (1985): 405-16.

Malina, Bruce J. 'The Social Sciences and Biblical Interpretation'. *Int* 37 (1982): 229-42.

Mayes, A.D.H. *Israel in the Period of the Judges*. SBT 2nd series, 29. London: SCM, 1974.

Mazar, Benjamin. 'The Aramean Empire and its Relations with Israel'. *BA* (1962): 98-120.

Mendenhall, George E. *The Tenth Generation: The Origins of the Biblical Tradition*. Baltimore: Johns Hopkins University Press, 1973.

Miller, J. Maxwell. 'The Elisha Cycle and the Accounts of the Omride Wars'. *JBL* 85 (1966): 441-54.

Miller, J. Maxwell and Hayes, John H. *A History of Ancient Israel and Judah*. Philadelphia: Westminster, 1986.

Miller, Patrick D. 'The Divine Council and the Prophetic Call to War'. *VT* 18 (1968): 105-106.

—*The Divine Warrior in Early Israel*. HSM 5. Cambridge, Mass.: Harvard University Press, 1973.

—Review of *Yahweh is a Warrior* by Millard C. Lind, *BA* 44 (1981): 188-89.

Miscall, Peter D. *The Workings of Old Testament Narrative* SBL Semeia Studies. Philadelphia: Fortress, 1983; Chico, CA: Scholars, 1983.

Moberly, R.W.L. *At the Mountain of God: Story and Theology in Exodus 32-34*. JSOT Supplement Series 22. Sheffield: JSOT, 1983.

Montgomery, James A. *Critical and Exegetical Commentary on the Book of Kings*. ICC. Edinburgh: T & T Clark, 1951.

Muilenburg, James. 'Form Criticism and Beyond'. *JBL* 88 (1969): 1-18.

Neff, Robert W. 'Saga'. In *Saga, Legend, Tale, Novella, Fable: Narrative Forms in Old Testament Literature*, pp. 17-32. Ed. George W. Coats. JSOT Supplement Series 35. Sheffield: JSOT, 1985.

Nelson, Richard D. *The Double Redaction of the Deuteronomistic History*. JSOT Supplement Series 18. Sheffield: JSOT, 1981.

Noth, Martin. *Die israelitischen Personennamen in Rahmen der gemeinsemitischen Namengebung*. BWANT, III/10. Stuttgart: W. Kohlhammer, 1928.

—*Das System der zwölf Stämme Israels*. BWANT, IV/2. Stuttgart: W. Kohlhammer, 1930.

—*Das zweite Buch Moses, Exodus*. ATD 5. Göttingen: Vandenhoeck & Ruprecht, 1959.

—*The Deuteronomistic History*. Trans. E.W. Nicholson. JSOT Supplement Series 15. Sheffield: JSOT, 1981. Originally published as: *Überlieferungsgeschichtliche Studien*. 2nd edn. Tübingen: Max Niemeyer, 1957.

Orlinsky, Harry M. 'The Tribal System of Israel and the Related Groups in the Period of the Judges'. In *Studies and Essays in Honor of Abraham A. Newman*, pp. 375-87. Ed. Meir Ben 'Horen. Leiden: E.J. Brill, 1962.

Overholt, Thomas W. 'Seeing is Believing: The Social Setting of Prophetic Acts of Power'. *JSOT* 23 (1982): 3-31.

Parzen, Herbert. 'The Prophets and the Omri Dynasty'. *HTR* 33 (1940): 69-96.

Pfeiffer, R.H. *Introduction to the Old Testament*. New York: Harper and Brothers, 1941.

Phillips, Anthony. 'The Ecstatics' Father'. In *Words and Meanings*, pp. 183-94. Ed. Peter R. Ackroyd, B. Lindars. Cambridge: Cambridge University Press, 1968.

Plöger, Otto. 'Die Prophetengeschichten der Samuel- und Königsbücher'. Dissertation, Greifswald, 1937.

Porter, J.R. 'מִדְבְּרֵי אִשׁ' *JTS* 32 (1981): 423-29.

—'The Origins of Prophecy in Israel'. In *Israel Prophetic Tradition: Essays in Honour of Peter Ackroyd*, pp. 12-31. Ed. Richard Coggins, Anthony Phillips, and Michael Knibb. Cambridge: Cambridge University Press, 1982.

Propp, Vladimir. *Morphology of the Folktale*. 2nd edn Austin: University of Texas, 1968.

Quell, G. *Wahre und falsche Propheten*. Gütersloh: Bertelsmann, 1952.

Rad, Gerhard von. 'The Deuteronomic Theology of History I and II Kings'. In *The Problem of the Hexateuch and Other Essays*, pp. 208-12. Trans. E.W. Truman Dicken. London: Oliver & Boyd, 1966.

—'Die falschen Propheten'. *ZAW* 51 (1933): 109ff.

—*Der heilige Krieg im alten Israel*. Göttingen: Vandenhoeck & Ruprecht, 1952.

—*Old Testament Theology*. vol. 2. Trans. D.M.G. Stalker. New York: Harper & Row, 1965.

—'Naaman: A Critical Retelling'. In *God at Work in Israel*, pp. 47-57. Trans. John H. Marks. Nashville: Abingdon, 1980.

Radday, Yehuda T. 'Chiasm in Kings'. *Linguistica Biblica* 31 (1974): 52-67.

Rehn, Martin. *Das zweite Buch der Könige: Ein Kommentar*. Würzburg: Echter, 1982.

Reiser, Werner. 'Eschatologische Gottessprüche in den Elisa-Legenden'. *Theologische Zeitschrift* 9 (1953): 321-38.

Rendtorff, Rolf. 'Reflections on the Early History of Prophecy in Israel'. Trans. Paul T. Achtemeier. *JTC* 4 (1967): 14-34.

Richter, Wolfgang. *Exegese als Literaturwissenschaft*. Göttingen: Vandenhoeck & Ruprecht, 1971.

—*Traditionsgeschichtliche Untersuchungen zum Richterbuch*. Bonn: P. Hanstein, 1963.

Rimbach, James A. Review of *Yahweh is a Warrior* by Millard C. Lind. *CBQ* 44 (1982): 297-99.

Robertson, David A. *Linguistic Evidence in Dating Early Hebrew Poetry*. SBLDS, 3. Missoula: Society of Biblical Literature, 1972.

—*The Old Testament and the Literary Critic*. Philadelphia: Fortress, 1977.

Robinson, John. *The Second Book of Kings*. Cambridge: Cambridge University Press, 1976.

Rofé, Alexander. 'The Classification of the Prophetical Stories'. *JBL* 89 (1970): 427-40.

—'Classes in the Prophetical Stories: Didactic Legenda and Parable'. *VTS* 26 (1974): 143-64.

—'The Story of Micah ben Imlah and the Question of the Genres of the Prophetical Stories'. (Hebrew) In *Reflections on the Bible*, vol. 2, pp. 233- 44. Tel Aviv: Don, 1976.

Rogerson, J.W. *Anthropology in the Old Testament*. Atlanta: John Knox, 1978.

Roth, Wolfgang M.W. 'The Secret of the Kingdom'. *The Christian Century* 100 (1983): 179-82.

—*Hebrew Gospel: Cracking the Code of Mark*. Oak Park, IL: Meyer Stone Books, 1988, forthcoming.

Sanda, Albert. *Die Bücher der Könige*. vol. 2. Münster: Aschendorff, 1912.

Schmitt, Hans C. *Elisa: Traditionsgeschichtliche Untersuchungen zur vorklassischen nordisraelitischen Prophetie*. Gütersloh: Gerd Mohn, 1972.

Schult, H. 'Naaman's Übertritt zum Yahwismus'. *Dielheimer Blätter zum AT* 9 (1975): 2-20.

Schweizer, Harald. *Elischa in den Kriegen: Literaturwissenschaftliche Untersuchung von 2 Kön 3; 6, 8-6, 24-7, 20*. SANT 37 (Munich: Kösel).

Scullion, John J. 'Märchen, Sage, Legende: Towards a Clarification of Some Literary Terms Used by Old Testament Scholars'. *VT* 34 (1984): 321-36.

Smend, Rudolf. *Yahweh War and Tribal Confederation: Reflections upon Israel's Earliest History*. Trans. Max Gray Rogers. Nashville: Abingdon.

—'Das Gesetz und die Völker: Ein Beitrag zur deuteronomistischen Redaktionsgeschichte'. In *Probleme Biblischer Theologie: Gerhard von Rad zum 70. Geburtstag*, pp. 500-509. Ed. H.W. Wolf. Munich: Ch. Kaiser, 1971.

—'Zur Frage der altisraelitischen Amphiktyonie'. *EvT* 11-12 (1971): 623-30.

—'Der biblische und der historische Elia'. *VT* 28 (1975): 167-84.

Smith-Florentin, Françoise. 'Histoire de la guérison et de la conversion de Naaman'. *Foi et Vie* 69 (1970) 29-43.

Snaith, Norman H. 'The First and Second Book of Kings: Introduction and Exegesis'. In *The Interpreter's Bible*, vol. 3, pp. 3-338. Ed. George A. Buttrick. Nashville: Abingdon, 1954.

Steck, Odil H. *Überlieferung und Zeitgeschichte in den Elia-Erzählungen*. Neukirchen: Neukirchener Verlag, 1968.

Sternberg, Meir. *The Poetics of Biblical Narrative: Ideological Literature and the Drama of Reading*. Indiana Literary Biblical Series. Bloomington: Indiana University Press, 1985.

Szikszai, Stephen. 'Kings, I and II'. In *IDB*, vol. 3, pp. 26-35. Ed. George A. Buttrick. Nashville: Abingdon, 1962.

Timm, Stefan. *Die Dynastie Omri: Quellen und Untersuchungen zur Geschichte Israels im 9. Jahrhundert vor Christus*. FRLANT 124. Göttingen: Vandenhoeck & Ruprecht, 1982.

Trible, Phyllis. *God and the Rhetoric of Sexuality*. Philadelphia: Fortress, 1978.

Tucker, Gene M. *Form Criticism of the Old Testament*. Philadelphia: Fortress, 1971.

Van Seters, John. *Abraham in History and Tradition*. New Haven: Yale University Press, 1975.

—*In Search of History: Historiography in the Ancient World and the Origins of Biblical History*. New Haven: Yale University Press, 1983.

Vater, Ann. 'Narrative Patterns for the Story of Commissioned Communication in the Old Testament'. *JBL* 99 (1980): 65-82.

Wallace, Ronald S. *Elijah and Elisha: Expositions from the Book of Kings*. Edinburgh: Oliver and Boyd, 1957.

Ward, J.M. 'Naaman'. *IDB*, vol. 3, p. 490. Ed. George A. Buttrick. Nashville: Abingdon, 1962.

Webster's Third New International Dictionary of the English Language. Unabridged edition. Ed. Philip Babcock Gove. Springfield, MA: G. & C. Merriam, 1969.

Weippart, Helga. 'Jahwekrieg und Bundesfluch in Jer 21.1-7'. *ZAW* 82 (1970): 396-409.

Weippart, Manfred. '"Heiliger Krieg" in Israel und Assyrien: Kritische Anmerkungen zu Gerhard von Rads Konzept des Heiligen Krieges im Alten Israel'. *ZAW* 84 (1972): 460-93.

Weisman, Ze'ev. 'The Personal Spirit as Imparting Authority'. *ZAW* 93 (1981): 225-34.

Wellhausen, Julius. *Prolegomena to the History of Ancient Israel*. With a reprint of the article 'Israel' from the Encyclopedia Britannica. Trans. J. Sutherland Black and Allan Menzies. Gloucester, MA: Peter Smith, 1973.

Westermann, Claus. *A Thousand Years and a Day: Our Time in the Old Testament*. Trans. Stanley Rudman. Philadelphia: Fortress, 1962.

—'Arten der Erzählung in der Genesis'. *Forschung am Alten Testament*, pp. 9-91. Munich: Kaiser, 1964.

—*Basic Forms of Prophetic Speech*. Trans. Hugh C. White. Philadelphia: Westminster.

Whitley, C.F. 'The Deuteronomic Presentation of the House of Omri'. *VT* 2 (1952): 137-52.

Wilcoxen, Jay A. 'Narrative'. In *Old Testament Form Criticism*, pp. 57-98. Ed. John H. Hayes. San Antonio: Trinity University Press, 1979.

Williams, James G. 'The Prophetic "Father"'. *JBL* 85 (1966): 344-48.

Wilson, Robert R. *Prophecy and Society in Ancient Israel*, Philadelphia: Fortress, 1980.

—*Sociological Approaches to the Old Testament*. Philadelphia: Fortress, 1984.

INDEXES

INDEX OF BIBLICAL REFERENCES

Genesis		2 Kgs 10	15 1n2	2 Kings	
1–11	14	8.14-17	83	2–7	53, 112
12–50	14	9.7	74	2	138, 139
				2.3, 5, 7,	15
Exodus		1 Kings			107n3
3	138	16.32	122n3	2.11-12	129
7.8-13, 20-22f.		17.6	138	2.12	92n1
	138	17.8-16	46n3,	2.16	107n5
16.4	39, 120		59n3	2.19-22	49,
16.8, 12	138	18	26, 59		111n1
19	138	18.20-40	138	2.19-20	46n3
33–34	138	19	138,	2.23-24	111n1
			141n2	3	45, 140
Leviticus		19.16-21	138	3.1-27	130
13	97n4	20	133,	3.9-19	133
14	97n4		134n2,	3.17-24	133
			141	3.18-24	140
Deuteronomy		20.13	133	3.18	133
17.16	140n1	20.15	133	3.27	140
18	136n2	20.35-43	133	4	121
18.15-18	139	20.35	107n3,	4.1-7	111n1
20	136n2		141n1	4.1, 38	107n3
31.14	138	20.42	141	4.1	107n5,
34.1-8	138	21	26, 121		122n1
34.9	138	22	133	4.5, 15	107n5
		22.5-23	133	4.38-41	111n1
Joshua		22.5	133	4.42-44	46n3,
3–4	139	22.6, 12, 15			111n1
5–6	139		133	4.42	42
11	140	22.10, 12, 14		5–7	12, 22,
			133		24, 29,
Judges		22.10	97n1,		30, 32,
7.22	98n3		103,		33, 36,
			125n4		63, 64,
1 Samuel		22.19	133n3		68, 149
1 Sam. 1–		22.23	122n3		

5	11, 22, 24, 28, 38, 42, 48, 56, 69, 107, 112, 118, 141, 150n2	5.21	81	6.11	86
		5.22	107n3, 122n1	6.12	86
				6.13-14	90
		5.23	81	6.13	87, 88, 91, 92, 93
		5.24	81, 82n3		
		5.25	82		
		5.26-27	144	6.14	87, 90n2, 91n2
		5.26	42, 83, 143, 145		
5.1-27	71-84	5.27	82	6.15-17	124
5.1, 3	73	6.1-7	70, 111n1, 122n1	6.15	88, 89, 91, 92, 144
5.1	76n2, 78, 79n5, 143, 145				
		6.1-3	107n5	6.16	89, 132, 140
		6.1	107n3		
5.2	42, 71, 73	6.2	107n5	6.17-18	132
		6.3	107n5, 113	6.17	89, 91, 110
5.3, 8	74				
5.3	72, 108, 114	6.6	42	6.18	89, 92
		6.8–7.20		6.19	90
5.5-6	114		121, 122, 125, 150n2	6.20-21	110
5.5	74			6.20	91
5.7-8	144			6.21	90, 91, 92, 126
5.7	75, 114, 119, 143	6.8-23	11, 22, 24, 28, 38, 42, 53, 56, 69, 84-94, 94n1, 109, 119, 138n2, 141	6.22	92, 93, 117n3, 126, 141
5.8	42, 75, 78, 83, 108, 114, 143			6.23	93, 95n1, 143
5.9-13	114				
5.10	75, 77n1			6.24–7.20	11, 22, 24, 28, 38, 42, 53, 56, 69, 95-104, 110, 138n2, 141
5.11	42, 74, 75				
5.12	76				
5.13	76				
5.14	73, 76, 77	6.8-10	86, 109, 125		
5.15	42, 77, 78, 115, 143	6.8	84, 143		
		6.9, 10	87, 88, 91	6.24	95n1, 98, 143
5.16	42, 78, 81	6.9	84, 85, 88, 109, 144	6.25	95, 97, 101, 126
5.17	42, 79				
5.18	79				
5.19	42	6.10	85, 123	6.26-33	96
5.20-27	48, 80	6.11-23	86, 109, 125	6.26, 30	99
5.20	79n5, 80, 81	6.11-14	122	6.26	99

Index of Biblical References

6.27	96, 97, 100, 103, 146	7.4	97	9.1	107n3
		7.3, 8	99	9.6-10	133
		7.6	97, 132	10.30	133
6.28-29	144	7.7	98, 141, 143	13.14-20	140
6.28	100			13.14-19	130, 133
6.29	98	7.9	96, 98, 103	13.14	92n1, 107n5, 129
6.30-31	144				
6.30	97n1, 126	7.10	102		
		7.11-15	123	13.20-21	111n1
6.31	96, 97, 98, 100	7.11	102	18.21-24	140n1
		7.12	100, 144		
6.32	98n1, 99	7.13	101, 102, 103	*Psalms*	
6.33	97, 98, 100			3.8	143
		7.16	99		
7.1, 16	144	7.17-20	102, 116n1	*Isaiah*	
7.1	95, 101			31.1, 3	140n1
7.2	99n3, 101, 113, 144, 146	7.17	100n2, 103	*Hosea*	
		8	26	13.4	143
		8.1-6	107		
7.3-20	96	8.4	107	*Matthew*	
7.3-4	103	8.7-15	46n3	8.26	145n1
7.3, 9	144	9-10	133		
7.3	96-99, 101	9	26		
		9.1-4	107n5		

INDEX OF AUTHORS

Ackerman, J.S. 131n1
Albright, W.F. 96n1
Alter, R. 70n1

Bach, R. 130-1n3
Barnes, W.E. 92n5
Beek, M.A. 139
Bentzen, A. 24, 25, 26, 27, 28, 29, 30
Berlin, A. 70n1
Blank, S. 107n6
Blenkinsopp, J. 130n3
Bostock, G. 151n4
Bright, J. 117-18n3, 122nn4,6, 128n2
Brodie, T.L. 151n4
Bronner, L. 37, 38, 39, 53, 62, 64, 117, 118, 119, 120, 147n2, 149n1
Brown, R.E. 31n3, 139n5, 151
Brueggemann, W. 32n3, 53n3, 61n4, 74n3, 80n2, 84n1, 86n1, 94n1, 97n3, 121n4, 149n4, 150n2
Buber, M. 130n3
Burney, C.F. 82n1, 92nn2,4, 130n1
Buss, M.J. 19n3

Campbell, A.F. 151n2
Carlson, R.A. 139n1
Carroll, R.P. 111n3, 138n4, 139
Childs, B.S. 57
Coats, G.W. 62n2
Cohn, R.L. 44, 61n5, 71n4, 73nn3,5, 74nn1,4, 75nn1,3,4, 76n2, 77nn3,4, 78nn2,4,5, 79nn4,5, 80nn2,3, 81nn1,2,4, 82nn3,4,5, 83n1, 150n2
Coulot, C. 139n1
Craigie, P.C. 135-6n5, 138n3
Crenshaw, J.L. 69n2, 111n3, 132n1, 135n2
Cross, F.M. 138n4, 141n2

Cross, F.M. and Freedman, D.N. 137n2
Culley, R.C. 46, 47, 48, 49, 50, 53, 65

DeVries, S.J. 32n1, 55, 56, 57, 58, 61, 62, 66, 111, 112, 113, 147, 149n3
Dietrich, W. 12n1
Donner, H. 129n2

Eissfeldt, O. 22, 23, 24, 25, 26, 27, 28, 29, 30, 61
Ellis, P.F. 31nn1,3, 107n2
Ellul, J. 57n2, 60n5, 61n4, 72nn1,2, 74n3, 76n1, 77n2, 79n2, 80n1, 96n3, 97n2, 98n2, 101n1, 103nn1,3, 110n2, 147, 150n2

Fannon, P. 31n1, 32nn2,3
Fohrer, G. 26, 27, 28, 29, 30, 1-30n35 135n4, 136n1, 138n4
Fretheim, T.E. 60n5, 61n4, 73n5, 78n4, 79n1, 82n5

Galling, K. 129n5
Gehman, H.S. 32n3
Geller, S.A. 151n1
Good, E.M. 69n3
Gottwald, N.K. 121n4, 129n2, 136n1, 149n4
Gray, J. 31nn1,3, 32nn2,5, 72n3, 84n1, 92n4, 96n2, 98n4, 99n1, 107n2, 130n1, 141n1, 147n2
Greenstein, E.L. 69n2, 70n1
Greimas, A.J. 47n3
Gressmann, H. 20, 21, 22, 23, 26, 30, 82n5
Gros Louis, K.R.R. 61n4
Gunkel, H. 11-68, 78nn3,4, 81n3, 106, 129n4, 130n1, 49

Hahn, H.F. 17n2
Hals, R.M. 34nn4,5
Haran, M. 151n3
Harrison, R.K. 71n2, 118-19n4
Heller, J. 37n2
Hermann, S. 117-18n3, 128n2
Hobbs, T.R. 60, 61, 62, 63, 66, 67, 72n3, 73n5, 75n2, 76n3, 77n2, 78n2, 80n2, 81nn1,2, 82n2, 83n1, 84n1, 87n1, 88n2, 92n3, 95n1, 96n1, 97nn1,6, 98n4, 100n1, 101n1, 102n3, 110n1, 118n4
Hossfeld, F.L. 111n3, 150n1
Hylmo, G. 24n5

Jenks, A.W. 128n1, 133n2, 138, 139n3, 141-42n2
Jolles, A. 34n4, 107n1
Jones, G.H. 44, 82n5, 85n1, 86n2, 135n5, 136n1, 147

Kaiser, O. 17n4, 18n2
Kaufmann, Y. 117-18n3, 128n2
Keller, C.A. 35n1
Kessler, M. 69n1
Kister, D. 36n4
Knierim, R. 58n3, 62n1, 69-70n3, 105n1, 147n1
Knight, D.A. 105n1
Koch, K. 29, 30

LaBarbera, R. 53n3, 61n4, 84n2, 85n2, 86n1, 89nn1,2,4, 90nn2,3, 91n2, 94n1, 97nn4,5, 99n2, 101n2, 102nn2,4, 119n2, 120n1, 121, 122, 123, 124, 125, 127, 149n4, 150n2
Licht, J. 61n4
Lind, M.C. 137, 138, 141n1
Long, B.O. 43n1, 45, 46, 47, 48, 49, 50, 51, 52, 53, 54, 55, 58, 59, 60, 61, 62, 63, 65, 66, 111, 112, 113n4, 121n2, 149n3, 150n1

Malina, B.J. 121n2
Mendenhall, G.E. 121n2
Meyer, I. 111n3

Miller, J.M. 122n6, 126n1, 129n1
Miller, J.M. and Hayes, J.H. 117-18n3, 129nn1,2
Miller, P.D. 131n1, 133n3, 138n3
Montgomery, J.A. 32n3, 79n5, 83n1, 92nn4,5, 96n2, 102n1, 130n1
Muilenburg, J. 69n1

Neff, R.W. 34nn1,3
Nelson, R.D. 12n1
Noth, M. 12n1, 135n3, 147n2

Overholt, T.W. 52, 112, 113, 115n1

Parzen, H. 122n5
Phillips, A. 92n1, 107n5
Plöger, O. 35, 36, 37, 39, 55, 59n3, 62, 64
Porter, J.R. 107n4, 130n2
Propp, V. 47n3

Quell, G. 111n3

Rad, G. von 72nn2,4, 74n3, 75n1, 80n1, 81n3, 89, 102n3, 108n2, 111n3, 130n1, 131, 132, 133, 134, 135, 136, 140n2
Rehm, M. 31n1, 32n2
Reiser, W. 36n3
Rendtorff, R. 130n3
Richter, W. 135n5, 136n1
Rimbach, J.A. 138n3
Robertson, D.A. 69n3, 137n2
Robinson, J. 31n1, 32n2
Rofé, A. 39, 40, 41, 42, 43, 44, 45, 55, 57, 59, 61, 62, 65, 108n1, 111n1, 149n2
Rogerson, J.W. 17n3
Roth, W.M.W. 152n1

Schmitt, H.C. 79n1
Schult, H. 77n3
Scullion, J.J. 13n3
Sellin, E. 26
Smend, R. 12n1, 131n1, 135n5, 147n2
Smith-Florentin, F. 75n5, 77n3

Snaith, N.H. 31nn1,4, 32n5
Sternberg, M. 70n1
Szikszai, S. 31n4, 32n3

Trible, P. 69nn1,3
Timm, S. 122n2
Tucker, G.M. 29, 30, 107n2

Wallace, R.S. 74n2, 79n3, 98n2
Ward, J.M. 71n1

Weippert, H. 135n5
Weippert, M. 135n5
Weisman, Z. 139n1
Wellhausen, J. 121n1
Westermann, C. 35n1, 36n4, 45, 47n4, 107n2
Wilcoxen, J.A. 20n1, 25n4
Williams, J.G. 92n1, 107n5
Wilson, R.R. 121n2, 126, 136n2

JOURNAL FOR THE STUDY OF THE OLD TESTAMENT

Supplement Series

1 I, HE, WE AND THEY:
  A LITERARY APPROACH TO ISAIAH 53
  D.J.A. Clines
*2 JEWISH EXEGESIS OF THE BOOK OF RUTH
  D.R.G. Beattie
*3 THE LITERARY STRUCTURE OF PSALM 2
  P. Auffret
4 THANKSGIVING FOR A LIBERATED PROPHET:
  AN INTERPRETATION OF ISAIAH CHAPTER 53
  R.N. Whybray
5 REDATING THE EXODUS AND CONQUEST
  J.J. Bimson
6 THE STORY OF KING DAVID:
  GENRE AND INTERPRETATION
  D.M. Gunn
7 THE SENSE OF BIBLICAL NARRATIVE I:
  STRUCTURAL ANALYSES IN THE HEBREW BIBLE (2nd edition)
  D. Jobling
*8 GENESIS 1–11: STUDIES IN STRUCTURE AND THEME
  P.D. Miller
*9 YAHWEH AS PROSECUTOR AND JUDGE:
  AN INVESTIGATION OF THE PROPHETIC LAWSUIT (*RIB* PATTERN)
  K. Nielsen
10 THE THEME OF THE PENTATEUCH
  D.J.A. Clines
*11 STUDIA BIBLICA 1978 I:
  PAPERS ON OLD TESTAMENT AND RELATED THEMES
  Edited by E.A. Livingstone
12 THE JUST KING:
  MONARCHICAL JUDICIAL AUTHORITY IN ANCIENT ISRAEL
  K.W. Whitelam
13 ISAIAH AND THE DELIVERANCE OF JERUSALEM:
  A STUDY OF THE INTERPRETATION OF PROPHECY
  IN THE OLD TESTAMENT
  R.E. Clements
14 THE FATE OF KING SAUL:
  AN INTERPRETATION OF A BIBLICAL STORY
  D.M. Gunn
15 THE DEUTERONOMISTIC HISTORY
  M. Noth
16 PROPHECY AND ETHICS:

ISAIAH AND THE ETHICAL TRADITIONS OF ISRAEL
E.W. Davies
17 THE ROLES OF ISRAEL'S PROPHETS
D.L. Petersen
18 THE DOUBLE REDACTION OF THE DEUTERONOMISTIC HISTORY
R.D. Nelson
19 ART AND MEANING: RHETORIC IN BIBLICAL LITERATURE
Edited by D.J.A. Clines, D.M. Gunn & A.J. Hauser
20 THE PSALMS OF THE SONS OF KORAH
M.D. Goulder
21 COLOUR TERMS IN THE OLD TESTAMENT
A. Brenner
22 AT THE MOUNTAIN OF GOD
STORY AND THEOLOGY IN EXODUS 32–34
R.W.L. Moberly
23 THE GLORY OF ISRAEL:
THE THEOLOGY AND PROVENIENCE OF THE ISAIAH TARGUM
B.D. Chilton
24 MIDIAN, MOAB AND EDOM:
THE HISTORY AND ARCHAEOLOGY OF LATE BRONZE AND IRON AGE JORDAN AND NORTH-WEST ARABIA
Edited by J.F.A. Sawyer & D.J.A. Clines
25 THE DAMASCUS COVENANT:
AN INTERPRETATION OF THE 'DAMASCUS DOCUMENT'
P.R. Davies
26 CLASSICAL HEBREW POETRY:
A GUIDE TO ITS TECHNIQUES
W.G.E. Watson
27 PSALMODY AND PROPHECY
W.H. Bellinger
28 HOSEA: AN ISRAELITE PROPHET IN JUDEAN PERSPECTIVE
G.I. Emmerson
29 EXEGESIS AT QUMRAN
4QFOLRILEGIUM IN ITS JEWISH CONTEXT
G.J. Brooke
30 THE ESTHER SCROLL: THE STORY OF THE STORY
D.J.A. Clines
31 IN THE SHELTER OF ELYON:
ESSAYS IN HONOR OF G.W. AHLSTRÖM
Edited by W.B. Barrick & J.R. Spencer
32 THE PROPHETIC PERSONA:
JEREMIAH AND THE LANGUAGE OF THE SELF
T. Polk
33 LAW AND THEOLOGY IN DEUTERONOMY
J.G. McConville

34 THE TEMPLE SCROLL:
AN INTRODUCTION, TRANSLATION AND COMMENTARY
J. Maier
35 SAGA, LEGEND, TALE, NOVELLA, FABLE:
NARRATIVE FORMS IN OLD TESTAMENT LITERATURE
Edited by G.W. Coats
36 THE SONG OF FOURTEEN SONGS
M.D. Goulder
37 UNDERSTANDING THE WORD:
ESSAYS IN HONOR OF BERNHARD W. ANDERSON
Edited by J.T. Butler, E.W. Conrad & B.C. Ollenburger
38 SLEEP, DIVINE AND HUMAN, IN THE OLD TESTAMENT
T.H. McAlpine
39 THE SENSE OF BIBLICAL NARRATIVE II:
STRUCTURAL ANALYSES IN THE HEBREW BIBLE
D. Jobling
40 DIRECTIONS IN BIBLICAL HEBREW POETRY
Edited by E.R. Follis
41 ZION, THE CITY OF THE GREAT KING:
A THEOLOGICAL SYMBOL OF THE JERUSALEM CULT
B.C. Ollenburger
42 A WORD IN SEASON: ESSAYS IN HONOUR OF WILLIAM MCKANE
Edited by J.D. Martin & P.R. Davies
43 THE CULT OF MOLEK:
A REASSESSMENT
G.C. Heider
44 THE IDENTITY OF THE INDIVIDUAL IN THE PSALMS
S.J.L. Croft
45 THE CONFESSIONS OF JEREMIAH IN CONTEXT:
SCENES OF PROPHETIC DRAMA
A.R. Diamond
46 THE BOOK OF JUDGES: AN INTEGRATED READING
W.G. Webb
47 THE GREEK TEXT OF JEREMIAH:
A REVISED HYPOTHESIS
S. Soderlund
48 TEXT AND CONTEXT:
OLD TESTAMENT AND SEMEITIC STUDIES FOR F.C. FENSHAM
Edited by W. Claassen
49 THEOPHORIC PERSONAL NAMES IN ANCIENT HEBREW
J.D. Fowler
50 THE CHRONICLER'S HISTORY
M. Noth
51 DIVINE INITIATIVE AND HUMAN RESPONSE IN EZEKIEL
P. Joyce

52 THE CONFLICT OF FAITH AND EXPERIENCE IN THE PSALMS:
A FORM-CRITICAL AND THEOLOGICAL STUDY
C.C. Broyles
53 THE MAKING OF THE PENTATEUCH:
A METHODOLOGICAL STUDY
R.N. Whybray
54 FROM REPENTANCE TO REDEMPTION:
JEREMIAH'S THOUGHT IN TRANSITION
J. Unterman
55 THE ORIGIN TRADITION OF ANCIENT ISRAEL:
THE LITERARY FORMATION OF GENESIS AND EXODUS 1–23
T.L. Thompson
56 THE PURIFICATION OFFERING IN THE PRIESTLY LITERATURE:
ITS MEANING AND FUNCTION
N. Kiuchi
57 MOSES: HEROIC MAN, MAN OF GOD
G.W. Coats
58 THE LISTENING HEART: ESSAYS IN WISDOM AND THE PSALMS
IN HONOR OF ROLAND E. MURPHY, O. CARM.
Edited by K.G. Hoglund
59 CREATIVE BIBLICAL EXEGESIS:
CHRISTIAN AND JEWISH HERMENEUTICS THROUGH THE CENTURIES
B. Uffenheimer & H.G. Reventlow
60 HER PRICE IS BEYOND RUBIES:
THE JEWISH WOMAN IN GRAECO-ROMAN PALESTINE
L.J. Archer
61 FROM CHAOS TO RESTORATION:
AN INTEGRATIVE READING OF ISAIAH 24–27
D.G. Johnson
62 THE OLD TESTAMENT AND FOLKLORE STUDY
P.G. Kirkpatrick
63 SHILOH: A BIBLICAL CITY IN TRADITION AND HISTORY
D.G. Schley
64 TO SEE AND NOT PERCEIVE:
ISAIAH 6.9–10 IN EARLY JEWISH AND CHRISTIAN INTERPRETATION
C.A. Evans
65 THERE IS HOPE FOR A TREE:
THE TREE AS METAPHOR IN ISAIAH
K. Nielsen
66 SECRETS OF THE TIMES:
MYTH AND HISTORY IN BIBLICAL CHRONOLOGY
J. Hughes
67 ASCRIBE TO THE LORD:
BIBLICAL AND OTHER ESSAYS IN MEMORY OF PETER C. CRAIGIE
Edited by L. Eslinger & G. Taylor

68 THE TRIUMPH OF IRONY IN THE BOOK OF JUDGES
　　L.R. Klein
69 ZEPHANIAH, A PROPHETIC DRAMA
　　P.R. HOUSE
70 NARRATIVE ART IN THE BIBLE
　　S. Bar-Efrat
71 QOHELET AND HIS CONTRADICTIONS
　　M.V. Fox
72 CIRCLE OF SOVEREIGNTY:
　　A STORY OF STORIES IN DANIEL 1–6
　　D.N. Fewell
73 DAVID'S SOCIAL DRAMA:
　　A HOLOGRAM OF THE EARLY IRON AGE
　　J.W. Flanagan
74 THE STRUCTURAL ANALYSIS OF BIBLICAL AND CANAANITE POETRY
　　Edited by W. v.d. Meer & J.C. de Moor
75 DAVID IN LOVE AND WAR:
　　THE PURSUIT OF POWER IN 2 SAMUEL 10–12
　　R.C. Bailey
76 GOD IS KING:
　　UNDERSTANDING AN ISRAELITE METAPHOR
　　M. Brettler
77 EDOM AND THE EDOMITES
　　J.R. Bartlett
78 SWALLOWING THE SCROLL:
　　TEXTUALITY AND THE DYNAMICS OF DISCOURSE IN EZEKIEL'S PROPHECY
　　E.F. Davies
79 GIBEAH:
　　THE SEARCH FOR A BIBLICAL CITY
　　P.M. Arnold
80 THE NATHAN NARRATIVES
　　G.H. Jones
81 ANTI-COVENANT:
　　COUNTER-READING WOMEN'S LIVES IN THE HEBREW BIBLE
　　M. Bal
82 RHETORIC AND BIBLICAL INTERPRETATION
　　D. Patrick & A. Scult
83 THE EARTH AND THE WATERS IN GENESIS 1 AND 2
　　D.T. Tsumura
84 INTO THE HANDS OF THE LIVING GOD
　　L. Eslinger
85 FROM CARMEL TO HOREB:
　　ELIJAH IN CRISIS
　　A.J. Hauser & R. Gregory

86 THE SYNTAX OF THE VERB IN CLASSICAL HEBREW PROSE
    A. Niccacci
87 THE BIBLE IN THREE DIMENSIONS
    Edited by D.J.A. Clines, S.E. Fowl & S.E. Porter
88 THE PERSUASIVE APPEAL OF THE CHRONICLER:
    A RHETORICAL ANALYSIS
    R.K. Duke
89 THE PROBLEM OF THE PROCESS OF TRANSMISSION
    IN THE PENTATEUCH
    R. Rendtorff
90 BIBLICAL HEBREW IN TRANSITION:
    THE LANGUAGE OF THE BOOK OF EZEKIEL
    M.F. Rooker
91 THE IDEOLOGY OF RITUAL:
    SPACE, TIME, AND STATUS IN THE PRIESTLY THEOLOGY
    F.H. Gorman
92 ON HUMOUR AND THE COMIC IN THE HEBREW BIBLE
    Edited by Y.T. Radday & A. Brenner
93 JOSHUA 24 AS POETIC NARRATIVE
    W.T. Koopmans
94 WHAT DOES EVE DO TO HELP? AND OTHER READERLY QUESTIONS
    TO THE OLD TESTAMENT
    D.J.A. Clines
95 GOD SAVES: LESSONS FROM THE ELISHA STORIES
    R.D. Moore
96 ANNOUNCEMENTS OF PLOT IN GENESIS
    L.A. Turner
97 THE UNITY OF THE TWELVE
    P.R. House
98 ANCIENT CONQUEST ACCOUNTS: A STUDY IN ANCIENT NEAR
    EASTERN AND BIBLICAL HISTORY WRITING
    K. Lawson Younger, Jr
99 WEALTH AND POVERTY IN ANCIENT ISRAEL
    R.N. Whybray
100 A TRIBUTE TO GEZA VERMES. ESSAYS ON JEWISH AND CHRISTIAN
    LITERATURE AND HISTORY
    Edited by P.R. Davies & R.T. White
101 THE CHRONICLER IN HIS AGE
    P.R. Ackroyd
102 THE PRAYERS OF DAVID (Psalms 51–72)
    M.D. Goulder
103 THE SOCIOLOGY OF POTTERY IN ANCIENT PALESTINE:
    THE CERAMIC INDUSTRY AND THE DIFFUSION OF CERAMIC STYLE
    IN THE BRONZE AND IRON AGES
    Bryant G. Wood

104 PSALM -STRUCTURES:
A STUDY OF PSALMS WITH REFRAINS
Paul R. Raabe
105 TEMPLUM AMICITIAE:
ESSAYS ON THE SECOND TEMPLE PRESENTED TO ERNST BAMMEL
Edited by W. Horbury

* (Out of Print)